ROUTLEDGE LIBRARY EDITIONS: MANAGEMENT

Volume 52

MANAGEMENT IN THE EDUCATION SERVICE

MANAGEMENT IN THE EDUCATION SERVICE

Challenge and Response

SOCIETY OF EDUCATION OFFICERS

Routledge
Taylor & Francis Group

LONDON AND NEW YORK

First issued in 1974 as an SEO Occasional Paper
First published in 1975 by Routledge & Kegan Paul Ltd

This edition first published in 2018
by Routledge
2 Park Square, Milton Park, Abingdon, Oxon OX14 4RN

and by Routledge
711 Third Avenue, New York, NY 10017

*Routledge is an imprint of the Taylor & Francis Group, an informa
business*

British Library Cataloguing in Publication Data
A catalogue record for this book is available from the British Library

ISBN: 978-1-138-55938-7 (Set)
ISBN: 978-1-351-05538-3 (Set) (ebk)
ISBN: 978-0-8153-6613-3 (Volume 52) (hbk)
ISBN: 978-0-8153-6618-8 (Volume 52) (pbk)
ISBN: 978-1-351-25976-7 (Volume 52) (ebk)

Publisher's Note
The publisher has gone to great lengths to ensure the quality of this
reprint but points out that some imperfections in the original copies
may be apparent.

Disclaimer
The publisher has made every effort to trace copyright holders and
would welcome correspondence from those they have been unable to
trace.

Management in the Education Service
Challenge and Response

Society of Education Officers

Routledge & Kegan Paul
London and Boston

First issued in 1974 as an SEO Occasional Paper
Revised, 1975
First published in 1975
by Routledge & Kegan Paul Ltd
Broadway House, 68–74 Carter Lane,
London EC4V 5EL and
9 Park Street,
Boston, Mass. 02108, USA
Set in Monotype Univers
and printed in Great Britain by
Unwin Brothers Limited
The Gresham Press, Old Woking, Surrey, England
A member of the Staples Printing Group
© Society of Education Officers 1975

ISBN 0 7100 8292 4

CONTENTS   PAGE

LIST OF DIAGRAMS   PAGE

MANAGEMENT IN THE EDUCATION SERVICE
CHALLENGE AND RESPONSE

PREFACE

During the past three years a group of Chief Education Officers and senior colleagues from local authorities and the Department of Education and Science have been meeting together on an informal basis to exchange experience on development in the management of the education service. The group was formed in 1971 as a result of the wish of officers of the Department of Education and Science and certain Chief Education Officers to exchange information and explore different approaches and techniques in planning at national and local level. The Society of Education Officers has agreed to sponsor the publication of this booklet so that the experience of these officers can be made more widely available. The views expressed do not necessarily coincide with those of the Society nor with the authorities served by the officers concerned. It is emphasised that the approaches to management in the education service outlined in the following chapters are only limited examples of new approaches in this field, and are still subject to development and refinement. They are put forward in order to focus discussion rather than to commend their immediate implementation by other authorities.

The officers who have contributed to these discussions are:

M. G. R. Adams	(formerly Gloucestershire C.C.)
Robert Aitken	(Coventry CBC)
J. F. Bolton	(formerly Liverpool CBC)
J. A. Brennan	(Coventry CBC)
E. W. H. Briault	(Inner London Education Authority)
J. D. Brierley	(Department of Education and Science)
D. G. Esp	(Somerset C.C.)
J. G. Evans	(Derbyshire C.C.)
W. J. Fenby-Taylor	(Inner London Education Authority)
G. C. Firth	(Coventry CBC)
H. K. Fowler	(formerly Derbyshire C.C.)
R. H. Gandy	(Greater London Council/Inner London Education Authority)
G. M. A. Harrison	(Sheffield CBC)
J. R. Jameson	(Department of Education and Science)
J. F. Mann	(Sheffield CBC)
J. H. Morris	(formerly Coventry CBC)
P. A. Newsam	(Inner London Education Authority)
R. M. Parker	(formerly Somerset C.C.)
C. W. Phillips	(Derbyshire C.C.)
B. E. Rodmell	(Department of Education and Science)
M. D. Shipman	(Inner London Education Authority)
B. Taylor	(Somerset C.C.)
J. Taylor	(formerly Somerset C.C.)

PART I INTRODUCTION

1. In 1970 there was some joy in the education service in the UK because total spending on the service in that year overtook spending on defence. The commitment of national resources was now second only to that devoted to health and social security. At last, education was assuming a proper place in the nation's priorities. In fact spending on education, both in cash terms and as a proportion of public expenditure, had been increasing steadily over the previous 20 years. Between 1959 and 1970 the average annual increase in expenditure on education was consistently higher than other public expenditure, higher than the increase in GNP and higher than increases in consumer expenditure. For example, in the decade 1960-70, 51% more was spent on education in real terms: yet only 10% more on food; 35% more on radio, television and so on; 44% more on alcohol (but 70% more on cars) (1). At the same time there has been growing pressure to devote more resources to some other public services, notably roads, health and social services. The rises in prices in recent years have also meant a rapid increase in consumer spending.

2. The priority given to education in the allocation of national resources is therefore being intensely challenged. First there is the pressure to control all public expenditure to bring its rate of increase in line with the rate of growth in the economy; second there is the need to recognise the demands of services other than education. The results of this process can be seen clearly in the annual White Papers on public expenditure published since 1969. These show: (a) that the overall rate of expansion for public expenditure has been reduced (3% in the 1969 White Paper; 2.7% in 1971; 2.5% in 1972; 2.0% in 1973); and (b) that the rate of growth for education has been changed relative to other services; for example, health and social services. (For education 3.8% in 1969; 4.5% in 1971; 5.0% in 1972; and 4.8% in 1973, compared with 3.8%, 5.1%, 4.8% and 4.6% for health and social services). This situation is reinforced by the legislation on Prices and Incomes and through the levels of rate support giants made by the government to local authorities. The impact of these factors is therefore that the flow of resources from government to local authorities is slowed down and redistributed somewhat between services and that, should a local authority feel the need to make up the difference, it can only do so by bearing the extra wholly on the rates.

---

(1) National Income and Expenditure 1971 and Glennerster "Willing the Means".

6

3. Translated to local level, this situation is posing some fierce problems to local authorities. Demand for services continues to increase fed by many factors: government legislation, social expectation, changes in the structure of the population, pressures for higher standards, rising costs. Indeed the cutback in public expenditure itself intensifies demand and needs — particularly among those consumers who are most vulnerable to rising prices. The creation of social services departments and related legislation (for example, the Children and Young Persons Act, 1969 and the Chronically Sick and Disabled Persons Act, 1970) have given a new impetus to the personal social services. Local authorities have considerable additional responsibilities in respect of services, not only for children (for example, intermediate treatment and assessment units), but also for care within the community of physically and mentally handicapped persons and the aged, representing a shift of responsibility from the health service to local authorities. There is continuing pressure for new houses and particularly for improvement of existing older properties or for the clearance and replacement of unfit property. This is reinforced by new powers and procedures under the Town and Country Planning Act 1968 which require the preparation of Structure Plans and declaration of local areas for action within the next 10 years. The rapid increase in car ownership and use of the roads produces demands for better traffic control, car-parking and standards of road maintenance. Environmental protection and improvement requires higher standards in sewage, industrial and domestic waste disposal, smoke control and drainage systems. Similar pressures are extending demands on the education service: for example, the 1972 White Paper "Education: A Framework for Expansion" which refers to expansion of nursery education, more places in higher education, better training for teachers and smaller teaching groups in schools. At the same time there are pressures for better provision in the youth and community services and for adult education.

4. The intensity of these problems will bear particularly upon the education service: (a) because, in the reorganisation of local government and following the redistribution of functions, the education service will tend to loom larger in the work of the county and metropolitan district councils responsible for the service; (b) because its share of the total budget of the local authority is between 50% and 60% and may be higher following local government reorganisation; and (c) because only a minor part of the education budget (at most 15%) is readily variable in the short term. About 85% of the budget is committed to staffing costs (teaching and non-teaching 65%), debt charges (12-15%), student awards and further education shared expenditure. The "vulnerable" 15% covers teaching materials, maintenance of premises and equipment, fuel and light, transport and administrative costs.

5. This situation is exacerbated by the structure and traditional approach within the education service. The standards of the service

7

have been built up over 150 years in the movement from local voluntary provision (largely by the Churches) through ad hoc Boards to local authority administration in a national system. Throughout that long process there has been a need to equalise standards so that now the provision required (for example, premises or teachers' salaries) is enshrined in detailed national regulations. This need to equalise standards has led to a concentration on inputs and to an attitude that equal standards of provision mean equal opportunities. This attitude is still apparent, for example, in pressures for smaller classes. The development of national standards, applied locally, has also meant that the service has attained a position of some isolation from other local authority services. At the same time, the education process is extremely difficult to evaluate and the crude measures applied in the 1860's (The Revised Code or Payment by Results) so frightened the service in this country as to leave a legacy of resistance to any form of measurement.

6. There are however good precedents for confidence that the education service can meet the present challenge. The adoption of national standards in the past has almost invariably followed the example set by local developments. Developments in a number of local authorities and within the education service are perhaps pointing ways in which the responses will be made. For example, three aspects in which this is discernable are:

6.1 positive discrimination: The Plowden Report advocated a redistribution of resources within the education service by the positive recognition that, because of the deprived circumstances of their situation outside school, some children require the deployment of greater resources in their schooling if their development needs are to be met as well as those of their more favoured peers;

6.2 strategic and corporate planning: local authorities have traditionally organised their budgets on an annual basis and according to the services they provide. This tended to obscure the relationships between services, inhibit joint planning and ignore the longer term effects of annual decisions on finance. There is now a strong recognition of the need to plan all services on a corporate basis and to present a coherent and comprehensive range of services to the public: for example, the inter-dependence of housing, social, planning and education services is clearly shown in the National Child Development Study "From Birth to Seven". There is an obvious need for joint development between education and social services and there are dangers of overlap in provision for under 5's, handicapped and maladjusted children, youth and community centres and intermediate treatment. As part of this process, an increasing number of authorities are developing policy and budget projections forward for 5 or 10 years;

6.3　effective use of resources: a number of authorities have taken steps to appraise their systems and to give emphasis to outputs rather than inputs. This has meant defining objectives and producing methods of analysing achievement and alternative policies. Changes in committee, departmental and financial organisation may also be involved.

7. All these matters present a considerable challenge to the education service. Pressures on resources means greater competition between sectors and services thus producing a greater need to justify, re-appraise and consider alternatives in the use of resources. These pressures are increased from within the education service itself, involved as it is with the whole age spectrum of the population and with the quality of life in our society. Under these pressures the standards, structure, organisation and fabric of the service are all under challenge. How can the response be made? The rest of this booklet describes various ways in which different aspects are being dealt with by a number of authorities.

PART II OBJECTIVES AND THE PLANNING PROCESS

Planning Paper No. 1 published by the Department of Education and Science recognised that "traditionally, budgets have categorised expenditure by the type of resource on which it is to be spent — staff, buildings, materials and so on — rather than by the purpose for which it is to be spent". That Paper went on to describe the feasibility of adopting an output budgeting approach which would seek "to analyse expenditure by the purpose for which it is to be spent and to relate it to the results achieved". Some Local Education Authorities have also been attempting to move away from the traditional approach. In doing so they have been faced with the need to define objectives for the service in their areas and to categorise activities which contribute to those object-ives. In this process new structures for the budget or programme of expenditure have been developed. The following sections compare the objectives and programme structures adopted in three Local Education Authorities and describe the development of the planning process at the Department of Education and Science.

(i) Programme Structures and Objectives :
   Coventry, Gloucestershire and Liverpool

1. The three major tiers of the education service are the Department of Education and Science, responsible for national policy, the local education authority which administers services within a particular area, and the educational institutions — schools, colleges and centres catering for the educational needs of particular groups. The Department of Education and Science can set broad objectives in areas such as comprehensive reorganisation, development of higher education or provision for under 5's, and plan the distribution of national resources accordingly. Such broad objectives affect the necessary level of inputs for the local authorities who have the task of achieving more specific objectives for their areas and need to provide *inter alia* the appropriate school buildings, an adequate number of teachers, and suitable equipment. In their turn these inputs by the authorities provide the constraints within which the school has to achieve its objectives. A hierarchy of objectives thus becomes apparent, from national to local institution level, each requiring its own set of performance measures. The Department of Education and Science review of teacher supply or Polytechnic development will mean little to the school more closely concerned with attendance, examinations and well adjusted pupils.

2. The concept of corporate objectives at local authority level is suggested in the Bains Report and to judge by the number of advertisements appearing for corporate planners, programme analysts and the like, many new authorities are now taking the Bains path to corporate management. Two of the management concepts already embraced by some authorities are Management by Objectives (M.B.O.) and Programming, Planning and Budgeting Systems (P.P.B.S.). Both require management to formulate clear objectives across the service as a first step to forward planning and resource decisions. Liverpool, Coventry and Gloucestershire have all espoused or courted P.P.B. to the extent of producing a programme structure. This involves the definition of objectives and the arrangement of elements and related activities under them in hierarchical form. A comparison of the programme objectives so defined reflects the different approaches and degrees of involvement of the three authorities in the new system.

   In theory the basic question of P.P.B. "what do we want to do and how can we best achieve it?" could be followed by a blueprint for a totally new administrative structure. In practice constraints of traditional procedures for accounting and accountability and limited resources result in a compromise — usually based on a re-ordering of existing systems. The process of setting and defining objectives then calls for a close knowledge of the existing work and organisation of the authority as a starting point for analysis, review and change.

The three approaches by Liverpool, Coventry and Gloucestershire to formulating objectives for the service vary quite considerably and point to real differences in the underlying assumptions made by each authority. While Liverpool takes its existing institutions as the starting point and has constructed its pattern of objectives and its programme structure around them, Coventry has concentrated on the different client groups that it seeks to serve. In contrast Gloucestershire has undertaken a fundamental rethink about the nature and purpose of education and produced a radically new set of objectives and programme structure dependent upon them (see Diagram 1).

3. Liverpool

The Liverpool programme structure is essentially "institution-based". The history of P.P.B. in Liverpool began when McKinsey and Co. were engaged as consultants by the Corporation in 1968 to prepare a new management system for the City. The firm's report recommended the adoption of a P.P.B. system for the whole of the Corporation's services and the Corporation set an extremely tight time schedule for its implementation. Programme structures were required to be worked out in a matter of a few months at the end of which time Programme Area Committees took over from the previously existing service committees and five year projections were produced. By the Autumn of the same year a Planning Budget, constructed on a programme basis from the projections of the new Programme Area Committees, was actually being made ready for 1970/71 and subsequent years, although for control purposes a traditional-type budget was also retained in parallel to it. Faced with the need to reorganise the pattern of the education service on a programme basis in so short a time the administration decided to accept as a starting point the actual pattern of ongoing work in the different institutions the authority was maintaining.

They identified the institutions on which the public provision of education in the city was founded as being:

3.1 The Schools

3.2 The School Meals Service

3.3 The Further Education Service

3.4 The Service for Children with Special Needs

To each of these four institutions, which they formed into the four constituent programmes of the "Education Programme Area", they ascribed a "Prime Objective". Programme 3.1 (Schools) and 3.3 (Further Education Service) were however so large that these two they divided each into Sub-Programmes but without separate Sub-Programme Objectives. Thus Primary Schools and Secondary Schools were seen as distinct Sub-Programmes of the Schools Programme and within the Further Education Service Programme,

12

the Liverpool Polytechnic, the Colleges of Education, the Colleges of Further Education, the Community Service and the Youth Employment Service were recognised as having separate Sub-Programme status.

The framework was next filled in by subsuming under each of the programmes groups of activities. An analysis was made of all the activities which were actually being undertaken across the whole width of the service and these were then arranged in more or less homogeneous groups and attributed to the programmes, each group of activities being regarded as an "element" and having an "element objective" attached to it.

The programme structure which resulted from this process (1) was thus a re-arrangement according to a logical pattern of all the ongoing activities of the local education authority at the time of the McKinsey Report. The objectives of the service were reached by inductive reasoning from a review of activities: if (so the authority argued) this, that or the other activity was ongoing in their institutions, there must be a final cause or reason for this being so which would be discoverable from a study of the activity itself.

A Liverpool philosophy of an institution-based programme structure thus came into being in contradistinction to the opposing philosophy which requires that the first question to be asked when embarking upon P.P.B. should be, not "why are we doing what we are doing?", but "what do we want to achieve and what ought we to be doing in order to achieve it?"

Since the somewhat hurried production in 1969 of a programme structure for education and the first programme budget for planning purposes, political changes in Liverpool, the onset of local government re-organisation and a rapid and progressive fall in the City's population have not merely inhibited further developments in P.P.B. but have actually led to a withdrawal from the position reached in 1970/71. After planning programme budgets had been produced for the years 1970/71 and 1971/72, a traditional-type single year budget was re-introduced for the subsequent years and the detailed five year projections formerly worked out were dropped. The programme area structure still however remains and its continued existence has proved useful in helping separate departments to work together in fields where the programmes of different programme areas overlap. It should also serve as a useful take-off point should more stable conditions return to the city and once more encourage the authority toward longer term planning of their services.

4. Coventry

In Coventry the adoption of P.P.B. formed part of a concerted effort by the Council to establish a system under which expenditure,

---

(1) See Appendix A on page 22

13

both capital and revenue, would be plannable over a much longer time span than had in the past been possible.

If such a system proved workable, short term developments would be able to be undertaken as deliberate steps toward the realisation of long term goals rather than as *ad hoc* improvements to meet current but possibly transient or ephemeral demands. P.P.B. was thus intimately linked with the drawing up of a Structure Plan for the City as a whole, within which plans for individual services and individual areas all found their appropriate places as elements of a grander whole.

The Prime Objective for the Education Programme Area was identified as being "to enrich the lives of the people by the optimum personal development of each individual in the community". Such an identification made essential the adoption of a "client-based" programme structure, the "community" being analysed into broad groups and the question having to be answered how for each group their optimum personal development was to be encompassed. *"Cui bono?"* was thus the question, whose answer determined in the end the shape of the programme structure. (1) So the School Meals Service, for instance, which in Liverpool is posited as a main programme within the Education Programme Area, was found in Coventry to be not a part of Education at all because it was seen as providing for the general benefit and wellbeing of the community as a whole rather than of school children *qua* pupils. Similarly Youth and Community services were seen as general services that the City provided for the benefit of the citizens at large and consequently more aptly grouped within the Leisure Programme Area with its wider orientation than in the personally oriented Education Programme Area.

One of the persistent difficulties that besets any planning for education is that the term 'Education' has no fixed and generally agreed interpretation even in the statutes relating to the subject.

Coventry, unlike Gloucestershire, chose for the purposes of their programme structure to adopt the narrow interpretation found for instance in Section 53 (1) of the Education Act 1944 where "persons receiving Primary, Secondary or Further Education" are referred to as forming a narrower population group than the general community. For Coventry the Education Programme Area has to do only with those forming this narrower group.

The client groups on which the Coventry Education programme structure is based are divided from each other mainly by age. One particular client group is however identified by a different criterion, that of being handicapped, and the members of this group may in fact be of any age up to 16. The groups identified, other than the handicapped children group, are the under 5's, children aged 5-11, children aged 11-16 and the over 16's. The programme

---

(1) See Appendix B on page 26

14

area, besides comprising a separate programme for each of these groups, also contains a general programme of Development, Research and Consultation.

As in the case of Liverpool an objective is assigned to each of the programmes within the programme area. The nature of these objectives is not however derived from a study of the on-going activities: they are expressed in very general terms most of which refer to the concept of "appropriate provision" for the client group concerned. The question "appropriate for what?" is invited and the answer is provided in the wording of the Prime Objective for the programme area as a whole, "appropriate for securing the optimum personal development of each individual".

Within the Objective set for each programme, Sub-Objectives are identified and the structure then lists the various activities which need to be and are undertaken in order to achieve these. The Sub-Objectives like the Main Objectives are couched largely in terms of appropriateness without attempting to define what scale of provision can for any given purpose be described as appropriate. In practical terms, the vagueness of what exactly is the optimum personal development of each individual and what activities are most conducive to its achievement has not inhibited the growth of a workable corporate system in Coventry under which the education services in common with other City services can be planned in a series of long term plans. In this system the undertaking of annual programme analysis exercises is not dependent on the measurability of progress towards the objectives and the authority find that they can in fact rationally allocate resources and choose between alternatives open to them without over-precision in defining either where they are going or how far along the path they have reached at a given point in time.

5. Gloucestershire

In July 1969 the County Council authorised a two year feasibility study into P.P.B.S. and set up an inter-departmental working party to carry it out. Programme objectives were defined and programme structures were developed as part of the exercise for seven areas, including Education: a report was made to the Council in 1971 and authority was given for the further development of the system with a view to its gradual introduction over a term of years.

By 1972 however there were already very clear indications that the new County that was being established under the Local Government Act of that year would not only differ substantially, despite its identity of name, from the old County but that there was a considerable body of opinion that thought the opportunity should be taken to establish with the new County a new and up-to-date pattern of management. Because of this the working party took a fresh look at the education service and made a new attempt at answering the question what education really is and what structure would best be adopted by the new authority for their education service in the light of what such fresh consideration revealed.

The new structure arrived at as a result of the fresh consideration given to the question by the officers' working party is based on the proposition that education is not in reality a single homogeneous service at all but rather a name given to a pattern of closely associated separate services operating through all of which is a recognisable motif — to promote and encourage the personal development of individuals. This group of services has been referred to as constituting the Educational Hemisphere of the Council's operations, being equivalent in financial and administrative terms to rather more than half the total effort of the Council.

Within the Education Hemisphere there lie three distinct programme areas. (1) These are referred to respectively as "Scholastic Services", "Vocational Assistance Services" and "Recreational and Leisure Services". To avoid confusion the word "Education" and its corresponding adjectival, verbal and adverbial congeners are deliberately avoided as much as possible in the programme structures, and are reserved for use in describing only their inter-relation with each other.

All three services are seen as services of assistance to individuals and their objectives are couched in terms that make this clear. That of the Scholastic Services is "to assist parents in the upbringing of their children...." ": that of the Vocational Assistance Service is "to assist young persons and adults to identify their personal aims in life and to earn their livelihood accordingly". The objective of the Recreational and Leisure Services is "to contribute to a high standard of civilised living by ensuring that opportunities are available to the community for exercising themselves both individually and collectively in artistic, literary, musical, aesthetic and intellectual pursuits of all kinds, in practical crafts and in sport and recreation".

Each of the three programme areas within the Education Hemisphere is divided (like the Education Programme Areas in Liverpool and Coventry) into a number of separate programmes. Scholastic Services and Vocational Assistance Services each have four programmes and Recreational and Leisure Services has six. A Research Programme and a General Administrative and Support Services Programme is included in each of the Programme Areas. Objectives framed in terms of the assistance to be rendered to individuals are ascribed to each of the programmes apart from the Research and General Administrative and Support Services.

An exercise undertaken during 1973 translated the traditional financial (input-based) budget of the old Gloucestershire Education Committee for 1973/74 into programme terms in accordance with the suggested programme structures for the three new pro-

---

(1) See Appendix C on page 29

gramme areas. This revealed that it would in fact be feasible to operate programme budgets on this basis given the necessary preconditions. No items of expenditure by the Education Committee are excluded from all three of the programme budgets but several items of expenditure by Committees other than the Education Committee were included in one or more of them.

Gloucestershire's approach is cautious. The time has not yet come when the elected members are prepared to abandon the traditional method of budget presentation. Nevertheless significant advances have been made and work is now proceeding on the possibility that, as a half-way house, an Options Budget might be produced covering at least some of the authority's programme areas to give Members the opportunity of determining future policy and resource allocation on the basis of an appraisal of alternatives derived from the P.P.B. approach.

6. Conclusion

All three authorities retain at any rate for the present the C.I.P.F.A. form of revenue estimates and the need to relate programmes and budgets to traditional accounting classifications is an evident constraint upon the definition of objectives in output terms.

Liverpool, and to a lesser degree Coventry, concentrate on inputs in the provision of staff, accommodation and materials. Activities parallel administrative functions and line estimates. To make the marriage of old and new systems work, the usual domestic compromises are made. Gloucestershire, as the authority least committed, is closer to the 'output' approach of P.P.B. theory. Areas of overlap, or 'cross-walks' with other services are identified and education is placed firmly in a corporate and community context.

General Administration and support services are put in a separate programme without stated objectives.

Different concepts and interpretations of education are highlighted by the comparison of objectives and structures. Age is the common criterion for separation of programmes but Gloucestershire have adopted a broader view of education than that of the two cities. While it firmly asserts that recreation, sport and community activities are activities related to education it provides a means whereby under cover of a very general education umbrella these services can be referred to a separate Committee from that responsible for the schools and the bulk of the further education work.

Liverpool considers the Meals Service sufficiently important to warrant a separate programme for it. Coventry just mentions meals at activity level, but, as has been pointed out above, regards the meals service as essentially outside education. For Gloucestershire the provision of school meals is part and parcel of the provision of schools. Again, in the sphere of provision for handicapped children Liverpool concentrate on placement in normal schools while

Coventry emphasises the provision of special schools and units. In Gloucestershire, on the other hand, where the authority's objective is defined in terms of assisting the parents, the programme structure indicates that this can be done, in some cases by providing for handicapped pupils in normal schools, in others by providing their own places in special schools and in yet others by helping the parents to send their children elsewhere.

The overall or prime objectives, couched in broad terms, represent the authority's creed or educational philosophy. Reference has already been made to a tendency to resort to such terms as "appropriate", "adequate", "suitable" and "optimim" when defining objectives, and the point should be made again here that such terms are less than wholly satisfactory in as much as they are incomplete in themselves and refer to unstated values and aims beyond them. The whole purpose for which P.P.B. systems are adopted is to aid authorities in decision making and in particular in deciding between alternative ways of attaining their ends. It is therefore of the greatest importance that the ends should be clearly defined so that progress towards them can be accurately monitored, and ends that by definition refer to remoter and vaguer ends beyond them, are liable to prove unsatisfactory as objectives to aim at.

The introspection, analysis and discipline required to formulate and set down objectives in an ordered structure has proved of considerable value to officers and members of all three authorities.

When Education Committees are now pressed by Policy and Finance overlords to justify their resource claims, and simultaneously colleges and schools are asking for less control and increased financial discretion, it seems not unreasonable for the l.e.a. to ask for a programme structure from its larger institutions. Staff, governors and parents could find this an enlightening exercise.

DIAGRAM 1

PROGRAMME STRUCTURES

(a) LIVERPOOL

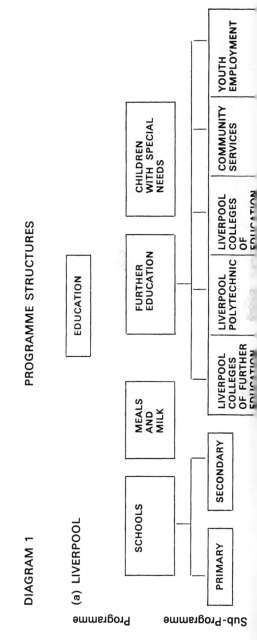

Programme

EDUCATION

Sub-Programme

- SCHOOLS
  - PRIMARY
  - SECONDARY
- MEALS AND MILK
- FURTHER EDUCATION
  - LIVERPOOL COLLEGES OF FURTHER EDUCATION
  - LIVERPOOL POLYTECHNIC
  - LIVERPOOL COLLEGES OF EDUCATION
- CHILDREN WITH SPECIAL NEEDS
  - COMMUNITY SERVICES
  - YOUTH EMPLOYMENT

(b) COVENTRY

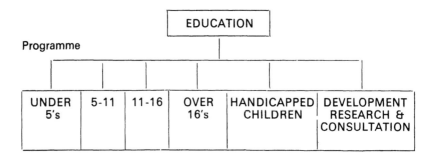

Programme

EDUCATION					
UNDER 5's	5-11	11-16	OVER 16's	HANDICAPPED CHILDREN	DEVELOPMENT RESEARCH & CONSULTATION

(c) GLOUCESTERSHIRE

EDUCATION is the name of a Hemisphere of the Council's services and the word is used to describe the relationship between the three Programme Areas within that Hemisphere — viz.

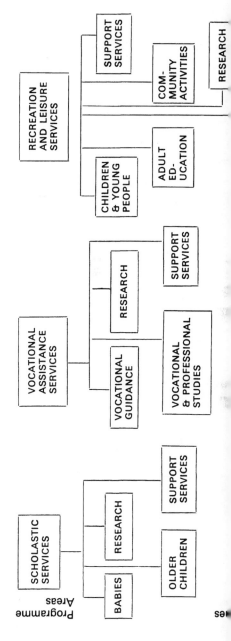

OBJECTIVES IN LIVERPOOL

Diagram 1(a) on page 19 shows the structure of the Education Programme Area. For each of the Programmes or Sub-Programmes there is a Prime Objective differentiated into Element Objectives and associated Activities. The SCHOOLS Programme provides a straightforward example of how the structure is put together.

PROGRAMME

SUB-PROGRAMMES

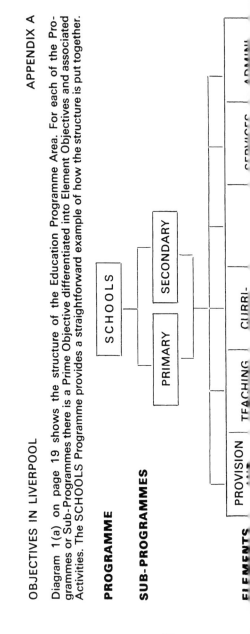

SCHOOLS

PRIMARY   SECONDARY

ELEMENTS   PROVISION   TEACHING   CURRI-   SERVICES   ADMINI-

SUB-PROGRAMMES

PRIMARY   SECONDARY

(Activities similar for each sub-programmes except where indicated:
*Primary activities
†Secondary activities only)

PRIME OBJECTIVE

To provide suitable full-time education for Liverpool children of primary* and secondary† school age whose parents wish them to attend maintained (county or voluntary) schools, and to make adequate provision for the needs of children below* above† statutory school age.

ELEMENT OBJECTIVE	ACTIVITIES
1. To provide premises that are adequate in quantity and quality for modern educational needs.	1.1 Assessment of pupil numbers and distribution. 1.2 Formulation of an appropriate organisational structure. 1.3 The design and improvement of new buildings, exisiting buildings and grounds. 1.4 To discuss provision for community use with other sectors of the service. 1.5 To provide furniture and equipment. 1.6 Maintenance of buildings and grounds.
2. To provide general and specialist teachers of suitable quality and quantity according to national standards and to deploy them to the best advantage. To provide support staff and material resources for teaching.	2.1 Assessment of pupils numbers and desirable staffing ratios. 2.2 To recruit qualified teachers according to need. 2.3 In association with governors and managers, to appoint teachers to individual schools within the overall policy of the Education Committee.

ELEMENT OBJECTIVE	ACTIVITIES
	2.4 To recruit and allocate non-teaching support staff; nursery assistants*, welfare assistants*, technical assistants†.
	2.5 Supply of material resources according to national standards: books; stationery and materials; and educational equipment.
3. To conduct research and development in the field of teaching method and practice and to propogate the material results thereof.	3.1 Establishment of suitable premises for research and development in both primary and secondary centres.
	3.2 Employment of appropriate professional staff.
	3.3 Employment of appropriate non-teaching support staff.
	3.4 Supply of material resources; books; stationery and education equipment.
	3.5 Organisation of in-service training: period secondment to attend extra-authority courses; and short-term secondment to attend Liverpool courses.
4. To provide school places to meet educational and parental demands not available within the normal provision of a Local Education Authority.	4.1 To negotiate reciprocal places with neighbouring L.E.A.'s.
	4.2 To provide selective places in direct grant schools.
	4.3 To provide places for specialist education in independent schools.
5. The provision of additional services to enable children to attend appropriate schools, engage in a variety of extra-curricular activities and travel for activities conducted away from the school site.	5.1 Provision of transport to and from school in accordance with local standards.
	5.2 Provision of fees and expenses in connection with the curriculum.

ELEMENT OBJECTIVE	ACTIVITIES
	5.3 Arrangement of outside activities to enrich the normal school curriculum.
	5.4 Provision of transport to schools and the Authorities detached establishments.
6. To provide adminstrative services in schools.	6.1 Employment of appropriate Clerical staff in accordance with locally determined standards.
	6.2 Adequate provision of stationery, telephones and administrative equipment.

OBJECTIVES IN COVENTRY

The objectives of the Education Programme in Coventry have been set out in terms of user groups differentiated mainly by age. The full statement of objectives, sub-objectives and activities is not reproduced here but the salient features of the approach should be apparent from the following extracts.

PRIME OBJECTIVE

To enrich the lives of people by the optimum personal development of each individual in the community.

This is then approached through six objectives:

OBJECTIVE 1

To ensure, in the light of parental wishes, adequate educational provision appropriate to the needs of infants below the age of five years.

OBJECTIVE 2

In association with parents and voluntary bodies to ensure the provision for all children other than handicapped children and aged between five and eleven years of full time education appropriate to their different ages, abilities and aptitudes and to their particular needs and to secure their participation therein.

OBJECTIVE 3

In association with parents and voluntary bodies to ensure the provision for all children other than handicapped children and aged between twelve and sixteen years of full time education appropriate to their different ages, abilities, aptitudes and other needs and to secure their participation therein.

OBJECTIVE 4

In association with other bodies (local, regional and national) to secure the provision of facilities for students over sixteen years of age to develop further their interests, skills and intellectual attainments to achieve the highest possible degree of competence and satisfaction in their vocation and in their personal life.

OBJECTIVE 5

In association with parents and voluntary bodies to ensure the provision for handicapped children up to sixteen years of age of full time education appropriate to their different ages, abilities and aptitudes and to their particular needs and to secure their participation therein.

OBJECTIVE 6

To ensure the progressive development of the education service; to identify the changing needs by the initiation and support of research; and to secure an effective consultative partnership of all participants within the service.

Each of these objectives is further broken down and the example of the sub-objectives and activities subsumed under Objective 3 will suffice to show the way in which this has been done.

SUB-OBJECTIVES	ACTIVITIES
3.1 To provide and maintain,with other bodies, a sufficient pattern of secondary schools appropriate in number, character and location.	3.11 The provision and maintenance of secondary schools.
3.2 In association with parents, governors and teachers and in accordance with the Articles of Government to ensure an appropriate standard and variety of instruction and training for all secondary pupils.	3.21 The provision of teaching staff for secondary schools. 3.22 The provision of educational materials to aid instruction and training. 3.23 The provision of inspection and advice to schools. 3.24 The improvement in the quality of the teaching force through in-service training and teachers' centres. 3.25 The encouragement of the development of educational thinking and practice through support for educational research generally and curriculum development in particular.
3.3 With parents to secure the regular attendance of pupils at school and to ensure that they are in a fit condition to benefit from the education provided.	3.31 The provision of facilities to improve the mental and physical health of all pupils. 3.32 Assistance in the transport of pupils to and from schools. 3.33 The provision of facilities to improve the standard of nutrition of all pupils.

SUB-OBJECTIVES	ACTIVITIES
	3.34 The provision of assistance so that no child is withdrawn from school because of financial difficulties.
	3.35 Improvement in the attendance of children at school.
	3.36 Enforcement of the regulations governing the employment of juveniles.
3.4 With parents, governors, teachers and voluntary bodies to ensure appropriate provision for extra-mural activities to promote the social and other development of children.	3.41 The provision of facilities for cultural development, outdoor pursuits and school journeys and outings.
	3.42 The provision of facilities for school clubs, hobbies and out-of-school sports activities.
	3.43 The provision of youth clubs and assistance to voluntary youth organisations.
3.5 To ensure that appropriate guidance is available to pupils concerning opportunities in Further Education and careers.	3.51 The provision of careers and educational advisory services.

Diagram 1(c) on page 21 shows the structure of the Education Hemisphere and the three Programme Areas within it. The next stage of the structure, the more detailed description of objectives and activities under the broad headings in Diagram 1, is exemplified by the following section which relates to the Programme for "OLDER CHILDREN".

The overall objective of the education service for children is

"To assist parents in the upbringing of their children in such a manner as to promote their proper spiritual, moral, mental and physical development".

In the case of older children, the objective is also

"To develop basic abilities and attitudes enabling individuals to become active members of society".

The activities or means employed toward this end are then described as follows:

1. By providing and maintaining schools.

   Costs to be broken down for each school by subject or groups of subjects. To include costs of extra-curricular activities when possible.

2. By maintaining schools provided by other bodies.
   As above.

3. By assisting parents with grants to enable them to send their children to schools not maintained by the authority (including schools maintained by other L.E.A.'s.)

4. By providing, and encouraging others to provide, facilities supplementary to school curricula.

   (a) Milk and meals in schools

   (b) Swimming facilities

   (c) Field centres

   (d) Museums

   (e) Short-term residential facilities

   (f) Children's libraries
       (i) Schools
       (ii) Community

   (g) Other facilities

5. By taking measures designed to enable children to derive full advantage from their education.

   (a) Identification of children with physical, mental or social handicaps and provision of advice and remedial measures.
      (i) welfare work and school attendance
      (ii) school medical service (part)
      (iii) school psychological service

   (b) Protection of school children from influences and activities harmful to their schooling.
      (i) restriction of employment

   (c) Financial assistance with costs of education for parents in need
      (i) school uniform grant
      (ii) grants towards costs of extra-curricula activities.

   (d) Transport between home and school.

6. By assisting and encouraging thinking about education

   (a) By providing and maintaining teachers' centres.

   (b) By enabling teachers and others to attend conferences, courses and seminars.

   (c) By making grants for educational research.

   (d) By grant aiding bodies having educational objectives.

   (e) By the services of a staff of organisers and advisers.

(ii) Educational Planning at National Level

1. The White Paper "Educational Reconstruction" of 1943 (Cmnd. 6458), the forerunner of the 1944 Act, had very little to say about planning the use of resources. It was mainly concerned with the statutory foundations on which the post-war education service was to be built. And for 10 years after the Second World War successive government and local authorities were struggling with limited resources to provide education on a scale sufficient to cope with the rapidly rising tide of numbers in the schools. Yet even that period saw the working out of the development plans for primary and secondary education required by Section 11 of the 1944 Act; the reshaping of the systems of special and further education; and the development of annual building programmes and cost limits which paved the way for large-scale educational building. If all this was mainly administrative, two important pieces of resource planning were the hutted operation for raising the school leaving age to 15 in 1947 (HORSA) and the emergency teacher training scheme.

2. By the mid-1950's the dismantling of war-time controls was complete and it became possible to develop an economic planning machine more appropriate to long term use. In education the first results of this were the 1956 White Paper "Technical Education" (Cmnd. 9703) which not only announced the designation of the colleges of advanced technology but also set out the planned level of capital investment in further education over a period of years. It was followed by the 1958 White Paper "Secondary Education for All" (Cmnd. 604) which described the Government's objectives of eliminating all age schools by 1965 and improving accomodation for the teaching of science — objectives which were substantially fulfilled by 1965 following the 5-year school building programme announced in that White Paper. Thereafter the pace quickened. The 7th and 9th reports of the National Advisory Council on the Training and Supply of Teachers (HMSO, 1962 and 1965) charted a course for an expansion of the colleges of education and an improvement in the staffing standards in the schools up to the 1980s. The Robbins Report of 1963 (Cmnd. 2154) made recommendations about the expansion of higher education up to 1973, which were accepted by the Government on the day of publication, and then to 1980 and beyond.

3. Although these White Papers and reports made valuable contributions to policy-making, they dealt only with individual sectors of the education service; and as a result they did not measure competing claims on resources. An important development was the acceptance by the Government in 1961 of the Plowden Report on the management and control of public expenditure. In 1963 the Government adopted a 4% growth rate as a target for the economy and all calculations of public spending were founded on

it. December of that year saw the first White Paper on public expenditure, covering the period up to 1967/68. (1)

4. The return of a Labour Government in 1964 gave new impetus to these developments. The new Government was concerned to plan national resources in greater detail than ever before in peace time and to try to relate its own policies, particularly for the social services, to the likely growth in the economy. Perhaps the pendulum swung too far and too fast; certainly many of the hopes of the National Plan of September 1965 (Cmnd. 2764) were dashed by subsequent events. Yet the education chapter of that Plan does not in retrospect look starry eyed, despite the succession of economic crises since 1965. Of the major objectives for education by the early 1970s laid down in the Plan, only the raising of the school leaving age — postponed for two years in 1968 following devaluation — was not achieved. The Plan, for instance called for a growth of 62,000 in the number of teachers in primary and secondary schools in England and Wales between 1965 and 1970. Despite unexpectedly high wastage rates during that period, the teaching force grew by 56,000. Again university numbers were projected in the Plan to reach 218,000 by 1973. In fact they reached 245,000. And the number of students in colleges of education in Great Britain in 1973, projected in the Plan at 122,000, exceeded 130,000.

5. In 1964 the former Ministry of Education had become the Department of Education and Science following the Conservative Government's rejection of the Robbins Committee's proposal for a separate Department responsible for higher education and science. The decision to bring together under one Minister responsibility for the whole educational process from nursery schools to post-graduate courses clearly facilitated the development of educational planning. The interaction of, for example, the supply of teachers for the schools and the growth of higher education was recognised in the administrative machinery at national level. And, with a Government committed to indicative planning through the National Plan, the Department moved formally into the planning business itself. A small Planning Branch, staffed by economists and statisticians as well as administrators, was set up in 1967, and by 1970, some of the results of its work became apparent with the publication of two education planning papers. EPP No. 1 (January 1970, HMSO) described the work

---

(1) For a fuller account of these developments see "The Developing System of Public Expenditure Management and Control" by Sir Samuel Goldman — HMSO 1973).

---

(2) For the more recent development of the programme budget, as it is now called, see Paragraphs 17-20.

done in developing output budgeting for the Department and included the result of a feasibility study undertaken in 1968. (2) EPP No. 2 (June 1970, HMSO) brought up-to-date the projections in the Robbins Report of the development of higher education to 1981. They have since been further revised.

6. The return of the Conservative Government in 1970 had important implications for the Department's planning machinery. First, the new Government came to office with certain political commitments, especially for the developments of nursery and primary education, which marked a change of course from the policies of their predecessors. Second, the new system of Programme Analysis and Review (PAR) was quickly adopted by the incoming Government as a contribution towards decision making. Following preparatory work by a group of businessmen based in the Civil Service Department, the Government decided to introduce a PAR system so that departmental expenditure programmes could be periodically brought under special review on a selective basis. Essentially PAR is a means of defining objectives, establishing alternative ways of achieving given aims, measuring more precisely the cost of the various choices available and analysing the results of expenditure of resources so that valid comparisons with costs can be made.

7. At the time of these two developments the Department's Planning Branch was wound up and new planning machinery was established. It rested on three principles:

7.1 Planning must directly involve those who must administer the policies that have to be planned;

7.2 Specialist skills must be built into the machinery in such a way as to ensure that they can make a creative contribution to policy formation without being able to determine it single handed; and

7.3 The planning machinery must keep close to Ministers, exploring among other options that reflect their known views and seeking Ministerial guidance and endorsement from time to time.

8. On this basis the Department's Planning organisation (DPO) since the beginning of 1971 has consisted of:

8.1 A Policy Steering Group under the chairmanship of the Permanent Secretary and including the most senior officials on both the operational and specialist sides. The role of the group is to determine the planning programme in consultation with Ministers, to trigger off particular planning exercises, to ensure that the appropriate planning machinery exists for the jobs in hand and to receive and review the results prior to submitting them, where appropriate, to Ministers.

8.2 Several Policy Groups, usually under the chairmanship of a deputy secretary, each directed to a major block of activities e.g. programmes and policies relating to schools, or to higher education. Each Group comprises a mixture of under-secretaries in charge of operational Branches and specialists such as HM Inspectors, statisticians, economists, architects, and cost accountants. Each Group is likely to break down into sub-groups to deal with particular aspects, but sub-groups are also established as integrated multi-skill teams.

8.3 A small Planning Unit headed by an under-secretary who is *ex officio* in membership of the Steering and Policy Groups. The function of the Unit is essentially to service the Steering and Policy Groups, to take the lead in preparing material in close co-operation with the operational Branches and the specialists. and generally to maintain consistency of methodology and co-ordination of effort across the whole departmental planning organisation.

9. With this new machinery, which also improved the Department's capacity to respond to changes in direction on public expenditure, and with the aid of PAR methods, it was possible to undertake a major re-appraisal of educational policies. This culminated in the White Paper "Education: A Framework for Expansion" of December 1972 (Cmnd. 5174). There was hardly a Branch in the Department which was not involved in this operation to some extent, although naturally the heaviest load fell on the main policy Branches and on Finance and Statistics Branches. Using conventional methods of calculation, the cost in manpower and supporting services was probably of the order of £150,000 spread over two years. The starting point for the operation was the known political commitments of Ministers, but a variety of options were explored in the course of the exercise, and the package which finally made up the White Paper of course took account of constraints on public expenditure generally. Because planning needs to issue in decisions and decisions must be negotiated through the public expenditure machinery, the Treasury was closely associated with the Department's planning operations. So too was the Central Policy Review staff, among whose functions is that of challenging spending Departments to consider new approaches and alternative methods of achieving objectives which their traditions of thought and procedure might otherwise rule out. By the time the results of the planning exercise came before Ministers for approval in principle in the early autumn of 1972 the two Central Departments were thoroughly familiar with them. Thereafter the drafting of the White Paper itself, though an arduous task for those closely involved, could proceed in the knowledge that the policies to be embodied in it had been subject to full discussions and analysis in Whitehall.

10. At an early stage in the operation it was agreed with the Central Departments that it must take as a starting point clearly defined objectives for the educational system, particularly for the schools. They were summarised as follows:

10.1   To enable children to acquire the basic skills of literacy, oracy and numeracy and to stimulate their curiosity and imagination,

10.2   To enable them to acquire the basic knowledge, practice in skills and in reasoning to equip them to enter a world of work which is becoming increasingly sophisticated in its processes and techniques, which is competitive, and which is likely to demand the ability to adapt oneself to learn new processes from time to time.

10.3   To leave children at the end of their period of compulsory schooling with an appetite for acquiring further knowledge, experience and skills at different periods in later life; and able to benefit from additional education to a variety of levels.

10.4   To prepare them to live and work with others in adult life; and to develop attitudes enabling them to be responsible members of the community: e.g. as parents and citizens.

10.5   To help them develop aesthetic sensitivity and appreciation: and skills and interests for leisure time.

10.6   To mitigate the educational disadvantages that many children suffer through poor home conditions, limited ability or serious physical or mental handicap.

11.   These are objectives which relate essentially to the individual and his personal development. But they also serve wider economic, social and cultural objectives. The economic objectives are concerned chiefly with increasing the country's productive capacity by providing a suitably prepared and motivated labour force. The social objectives relate to the attitudes which the young will have formed by the time they become adult members of the community: attitudes toward each other and toward society as a whole. The cultural objectives concern the transmission of a common culture: the scientific and artistic heritage of our society, whether in scholarly or practical forms.

12.   The attainment of these objectives is powerfully influenced by other factors in society:

12.1   The family: probably the most influential single factor and the most difficult to influence. Ideally the home will preserve the integrity of the family unit (mother, father and children remaining an intact group) and provide affection, economic stability employment and common sense in money matters and a certain level of parental education and culture. Government policy affects the last two.

12.2   Health: the health services share common objectives with education in the early years of a child's life, when physical development is particularly rapid. The transfer of the School Health Service to the National Health Service will require new co-operative efforts at both national and local level.

12.3 Deprivation: the personal social services share objectives with education in relation to those children — and their parents — who suffer from personal or social deprivation.

12.4 Physical environment: this ranges from the quality of individual houses to the nature of the whole neighbourhood. Urban planning, estate layout, rural housing, the physical relationship between house, school, shops, transport, social and cultural facilities, are all involved.

12.5 The mass media: television, in particular, exerts a powerful and persuasive influence. It almost certainly conditions moral and behavioural standards more than formal education does.

13. Thus education operates as one force in a field of forces, some of which are affected by other aspects of government policy. There is close interplay between education and other relevant areas of social policy. While education can support the objectives of these other social policies, the latter exert their own increasingly significant influence on the total environment within which the educational process takes place — and therefore on the results of this process.

14. Three further general conclusions may be drawn. First, educational policies usually serve more than one educational objective. Second, most educational policies serve some or all of the educational objectives set out above. Third, while educational objectives tend to predominate in determining most educational policies, the latter also serve other objectives. It will be apparent that the balance of educational, social and economic elements varies in relation to different parts of the educational system and to different options within them. Higher education objectives are partly educational or personal and partly social or economic. The organisation of the secondary school system (even the internal organisation of an individual school) serves partly social and partly educational objectives. Similarly, the case for an expansion of nursery provision, while it rests primarily on educational considerations, has subsidiary social objectives.

15. All these factors played their part in the planning process. The White Paper which emerged from it was subjected to a good deal of detailed criticism. But most commentators welcomed the evidence in it of the Government's determination to review in detail something like three quarters of educational expenditure and to make clear choices affecting five major areas of policy. In other countries too the educational planning process was becoming more sophisticated. In the autumn of 1973 the Federal Government and the Länder in West Germany approved a plan for education to 1985 which contained many familiar features — a big expansion of nursery and higher education, for instance, and a marked improvement in primary school staffing standards.

16. During 1973 the Department's planning machinery was engaged in revising and extending the projections in the White Paper in the light of new data (for example about the projected school population and the demand for higher education). When the Government made major reductions in December 1973 in the level of public expenditure previously planned for 1974/75 it was therefore possible to try to distribute the cuts affecting the education service in such a way as to do least damage to the objectives of the White Paper. Thus the plans for nursery education, in-service training and teacher supply have been largely protected; and the curtailment of the rate of growth of higher education does not necessarily mean the abandonment of the White Paper policy. That policy was to provide places for those able and willing to take them up; and the latest indications are that the proportion of those qualified for higher education who wish to take up places is falling. By the autumn of 1973 there were grounds for believing, with another year's experience of the trends, that the planning figure of 750,000 higher education places in the White Paper was too large.

17. The establishment of the DPO has been accompanied by development of the Department's programme budget. As mentioned earlier, work on this had begun in the former Planning Branch, and following the 1968 Feasibility Study (published 1970) a decision had been taken to work towards annual calculation of programme budgets to help in understanding the growth of educational expenditure. By 1971 therefore, when the DPO was set up, there had been two attempts at producing operational programme budgets, and although they were still not very fully developed analytically, they did provide a reference framework against which the new Policy Groups could examine alternative strategies. The DPO effectively performs the second and third functions of a classical programme budget system — the review of policy objectives in the light of progress towards their attainment to check their continuing validity, and the identification of areas in which special studies are needed. As such, it is the main prospective user of the programme budget, even though it has not drawn directly upon the budget to the extent originally expected.

18. The contribution of the programme budget to the Department's planning activity has been more indirect — as a preliminary guide to relative magnitudes in the educational expenditure field, and as a quarry from which partly-processed data could be extracted. The former was probably the more important contribution at the start of the PAR process, when an understanding of relative magnitudes was needed to help in deciding the general orientation of the work. The programme budget has been designed to show the determinants of educational expenditure — how much was needed merely to maintain standards in the face of population increase, how much arose from growth in the numbers choosing to participate in education, how much would be needed to accomplish

planned improvements in the system. Other analyses within the programme budget showed the relative importance of various institutions at each level of education, and the share of expenditure attributable to various resource inputs (teachers, other staff, building, etc.). It thus helped to inform the new Policy Groups about the limits within which alternative policies could meaningfully be considered.

19. As the PAR work proceeded, the role of the programme budget became more that of a quarry for data. Its value for this purpose arose partly from being based on more detailed unit costs and statistical projections than were used for 5-year public expenditure projections, partly from the time-span of these projections, for the programme budget calculations were being advanced from a 5-year to a 10-year span at about the time the PAR work, which also required 10-year projections, was getting under way. Somewhat different calculations were often required for PAR purposes, where the need was more for costing possible alternative policies than for the analysis of existing policy provided by the programme budget. Nevertheless, the economists and statisticians supporting the Policy Groups were able to draw substantially on the worksheets underlying the programme budget to simplify the task of producing alternative expenditure projections.

20. The advantages of partly-processed figures stem from the amount of manipulation needed to convert raw data into something usable for planning purposes. Statistical returns from local authorities and elsewhere relate to an assortment of dates, or to academic years, and have all to be converted to a financial year basis for combination with financial returns. Figures on an institutional basis have to be broken down and recombined to show provision at various levels of education. Projections for future years have to be drawn from trends based on historical data, adjusted as necessary for known changes in circumstances and revised annually as new statistics arrive. Expenditure projections prepared for other purposes have to be broken down into their components of existing services, provision for growth, improvements, etc. So far all of this work has had to be undertaken within DES because the information received from local authorities, universities and other spending bodies is not in the form needed for planning use. As local authorities develop more comprehensive planning functions they may well require more information in this form for their own use — particularly those authorities adopting a programme budget approach — and this should lead to interchanges of data extending beyond the existing statistical returns.

21. Another potential form of co-operation between central and local government is in assessment of the results of different kinds of educational provision. So far the Department's educational planning has been largely concerned with the planning of inputs — of money, buildings, teachers, etc. Additional resources have been

provided in the belief (based on informed advice) that improved education would follow, but there has been little opportunity for systematic comparison of the effects of different kinds of provision. Indeed, this would be impossible for the Department alone to undertake on any meaningful scale. This is an area that local authorities are better placed to explore, and their participation in this offers one of the most promising ways of achieving a closer link between local and national planning.

22. Several conclusions emerge from the development of educational planning so far. First, the practice of showing expenditure on components of the education budget to within £1m up to 10 years ahead must not mislead anyone about the degree of uncertainty that must enter into long-term estimates of this kind. Although education is a service whose planning is heavily dependent on sheer numbers, and the collection of reliable and useful data has been highly developed, the degree of uncertainty and therefore of risk taking in educational planning remains substantial and projections must be constantly revised and extended — as in 1973. Second, because of the time-lags, resistances and frictions in the system, major changes of direction and pace can be achieved only slowly. Most of what is going to happen in the next five years is largely determined already; and in a ten-year look ahead the real room for change lies only in the second five years — in the next Parliament but one.

23. A final important conclusion to be drawn from the experience since 1971 is that it is a mistake to confine too narrowly within the Department the thinking that underlies the plans before they are published. This is a particular problem of planning in the education service where the balance of power and influence between central government, local government and the academic and professional worlds has been carefully drawn. Ways must be found of associating these other parties and the local authority associations more closely with the planning process, the results of which are often vital to their interests. There are great difficulties about this — the size of the planning machinery that will be necessary; the increased area of potential conflict, making decision taking on critical time-tables more difficult; the responsibilities which Ministers cannot delegate; and the inevitable confidentiality, not so much of the data itself, but of the economic and political background to policy formation. But the development of participative planning is a direction in which the Department is seeking to move where it can. The establishment of the Advisory Committee on the Supply and Training of Teachers is one example; and the reorganisation of local government into larger units, together with any development of regional bodies that may flow from the report of the Commission on the Constitution, may in time provide opportunities for further initiatives.

PART III ORGANiSATION

The development of new approaches in the planning process has led to changes of organisation both at national and local government levels. Those at national level were described in the previous section. Some local authorities have adopted corporate management systems involving all services and departments in a multi-disciplinary approach. Changes of organisation within the Education Department of a local authority have also occurred and these developments in two authorities are described below.

(i)   Matrix Management — Sheffield

1.   The Local Government Act, 1972 is a first class catalyst. In our
     case four or five years of self exmaination was brought to a
     successful conclusion by the imminence of 1st April, 1974. Our
     otherwise interminable analysis of aims, objectives, structures and
     systems was quickly ended when we turned to the practical prob-
     lem of trying to get a sensible establishment for the new authority.
     Most of this chapter is about the stage of development now
     reached, but a glance at the factors which stimulated change may
     be of interest. We enjoyed the classic change agents, lengthy
     courses for the Chief and Deputy Education Officers and then for
     many others, and the services of committed consultants with a
     gospel of analysis and review. We suffered too from the territorial
     imperative as we struggled to assimilate two new third tier posts
     to the three we previously had.

2.   This is not the place to describe the trauma of self analysis and
     change. What does matter is that our analysis led us to recognise
     that the Department makes three main contributions to the educa-
     tion service. First is the development of policies and strategic
     planning, second the implementation of policies, and third monitor-
     ing the effect of policies and discovering consumers' needs.

     Our conclusion has marked similarities to that of F. J. C. Amos,
     City Planning Officer of Liverpool. (1).

     'The essential need is to create a structure in which there can be
     a high degree of professional competence coupled with flexi-
     bility of operation. Perhaps the best way of achieving these two
     qualities would be to maintain (or establish as necessary)
     departments of professional competence, but separately to
     create programmes and project directorates which would devise
     and manage programmes to achieve specified objectives.'

     In our case the recognition of not two but three functions led us
     to create a 3-D matrix organisation. The development of policies
     and strategic planning is undertaken by a team of a dozen Pro-
     gramme Managers. Policies are implemented by Functional
     Managers, each of whom heads an executive branch which also
     undertakes day-to-day administration, the need for which arises
     of course from now forgotten policy decisions of another age.
     Finally, Field Officers assess the effects of policies, discover
     consumer needs and represent those needs at the centre. In its own
     way each group is responsible for facets of the whole education
     service; it is the interaction of the three groups with each other
     and with their external contacts which constitutes the matrix.

(1)   In 'Planning strategies and implementation', Town and Country
      Planning Summer School, Southampton, 1971 :

DIAGRAM 2   THE SHEFFIELD MATRIX

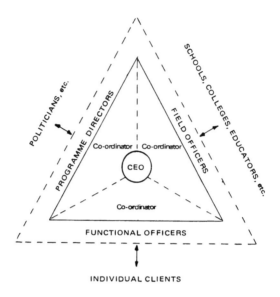

INDIVIDUAL CLIENTS

The structure of relationships within the department as a pyramid seen from above. Functional Officers, Programme Directors and Field Officers work together within the structure.

3. Though grades and salaries differ somewhat between groups and within each group, there is intended to be no order of precedence between groups, and no hierarchy at the senior level inside each group. From brief experience of our matrix we can confirm the view expressed by Greenwood and Stewart that "matrix organisations reduce the importance of extrinsic rewards". (1). Differences in salary levels have not been the cause of any objection to the introduction of matrix management though we do not regard that as a reason for not changing them later.

4. The need for leadership and co-ordination of the three teams is recognised. The deputy education officer is co-ordinator of the Programme Managers, and among the Programme Managers are the former senior assistant education officer (administration) who

(1)   'Corporate Planning and Management Organisation', Local Government Studies, October 1972.

supervises the Functional Managers, and the former senior adviser who co-ordinates the Field Officers. And lest it be thought that the establishment is prodigal, please note that several officers wear two or even three hats as members of more than one group. The Principal Careers Officer and the Principal Educational Psychologist for example each wear three, as policy developers, as managers of small branches, and as leaders of fieldwork teams.

Initiatives are expected to come from any of the three groups. If a Field Officer or Functional Mangaer's experience leads him to ask a question which indicates an absence of promulgated general principles the appropriate Programme Manager is expected to formulate a policy statement, which may have to be referred to Committee. In formulating policy statements on major issues the Programme Manager will probably need to call on the help of several Functional Managers, or Field Officers. Similarly, Field Officers may relate direct to the Functional Branches or *vice versa*.

5. In considering what programme areas to define we were tempted to use the traditional ages and stages of education which are the basis of the Department of Education and Science's work in output budgeting. By themselves, however, these seemed inadequate. We recognised a need to take an overall view of personal policies, the needs of the handicapped and the disadvantaged, and of post-16 education whether in school or college, to respond to major short term problems like school reorganisation, and entry to the Common Market, to develop policies on relations with other corporation departments, publicity, safety and other issues, and to recognise that catering, health, guidance and welfare services could be thoroughly integrated only if the officers in charge of these services participated in the collective development of policies. In defining programme areas and appointing for each an accountable Programme Manager we have therefore deliberately built in over-lap and some double banking, to emphasise that our programmes are mutually dependent.

The result is a statement of programmes much longer and more precise than the traditional list of education department branches, and more extensive than the modern programme budgeting strait-jacket. Indeed, some of the items we regard as important enough to stand on their own would need only a few hours of a senior man's time, and barely a line in any kind of budget. This may be because we are as much concerned with increasing the effective-ness of the process of education and management, as with the size of the inputs. A few of our programmes are of purely local concern, and another group correspond to some extent with the functional branches:

Programme Areas	Corresponding Functional Branches

Ages and Stages
Pre school
5-8
8-12
Secondary schools
Post 16 (excluding higher and community education) — Educational establishments
Campuses
Community education
Higher education
Education of the handicapped
Education of the disadvantaged
Pupil counselling and human relations

Functions
Curriculum development
Property development (Schools)
Property development (higher and community education, branch colleges) — Premises and land
Teaching resources, equipment and materials
Teaching staff — Supplies
Non-teaching staff — Staffing

Major Projects
Roman Catholic reorganisation
Local government reorganisation
Rowlinson Campus Project
Earl Marshal Campus Project
Reorganisation of schools (excluding RC)
Education priority areas
Mosborough Satellite town development

External Relations
Corporation departments
Examination boards
Research organisations
Press and publicity
Committee — Committee and office services

Central Services
Careers service — Careers service
Psychological service — Psychological service
Pupil services
Catering — School Meals service
Health — (a) School Health service
(b) Child guidance
Computer applications (administrative)
Resource management — Management accounting
Organisational and departmental management
Security, safety and fire

In all we have defined almost forty programme areas, so on average each Manager is accountable for three or four areas which are not necessarily closely related to each other.

6. It would clearly be difficult to work with as many as forty Functional Branches, and the existence of overlaps would be an embarrassment, not a strength, in day-to-day administration. We have created only eleven Branches, four corresponding to the traditional Careers, Health, Psychological and Meals Services, and seven others, Staffing, Supplies, Financial accounting, Management Accounting, Premises and Land, Educational Establishments, and Committee and Office services. The traditional Schools, Special Services and Further Education Branches have disappeared.

   These seven handle all financial matters and virtually all routine matters leaving only the professional elements of the Careers, Health, Psychological and Meals Services to be handled in these specialist branches.

7. The professionals working in the four latter services are of course an important part of the force of Field Officers, who also include Welfare Officers, Youth Officers, Adult Organisers, and Advisers. Sometimes the Field Officers operate in their traditional professions, but at other times it is better for them to turn their searchlight on a particular stage of education, a subject area, or a district in the city. They must be free, as the Programme Managers are, to form and reform in whatever pattern is appropriate, creating a matrix within the matrix.

8. The essence of this system was agreed in the late spring 1972, and the decision was then taken to introduce matrix management as soon as possible. Most of the Programme Managers took on their role in July, and the Functional Branches began to operate in September. The system has been fully operative from 1st December, 1972.

9. The matrix undoubtedly increases responsibility. The P.M.s are accountable for developing policies in certain defined areas, and are free to concentrate on this important work. The F.M.s are wholly accountable for implementing policies, including the monitoring and control of expenditure. The F.O.s have a clear and significant role. In a sense the matrix has meant job enlargement for all the senior officers. It certainly seems to have created high morale and increased commitment.

   From the viewpoint of a departmental manager the new organisation is easier and simpler to use, because it is almost always possible to pinpoint the one senior officer who is accountable for initiating action on any question.

   The Programme Managers share among them for example, accountability for achieving the department's objectives and their performance can be measured against their achievements of these objectives. Similarly the performance of the functional managers can be compared with the agreed statement of the managers' task. Once the new system has settled down it will be possible to introduce performance standards and fairly orthodox MBO to the functional branches.

Above all we are finding it increasingly easy to nominate and to mobilise expertise in the preparation of major reports. Almost as a matter of course whenever we meet to tackle a complex problem our task force is drawn from all three parts of the matrix.

Already we feel confident enough in the management techniques we are developing in mobilising our own heterogeneous groups to have offered our experience to inter-departmental groups considering the social problems and development of various parts of the city.

10. We also feel that we have solved half a dozen problems which bugged the pre-matrix organisation:

10.1 The colossal accountability of the Senior AEOs (Schools and F.E.) who were supposed to initiate policies, oversee a budget, and manage both a branch and many schools or colleges.

10.2 Our difficulties in coping with problem areas which fell outside the strict accountability of any one branch (Schools or F.E.), such as 16-19 education, the handicapped or a major community project.

10.3 Several small units within Branches were engaged in essentially the same kind of day-to-day administration.

10.4 Difficulty of anyone below chief or deputy taking an overall view.

10.5 Lack of role description which gave the advisers job satisfaction.

10.6 Absence of a system for profiting from the experiences and knowledge of many, such as careers officers, psychologists, doctors, nurses and welfare officers, whose work regularly brings them into touch with pupils, teachers and parents.

In resolving these difficulties we have done much to remove inefficiency and frustration.

11. There are of course a number of unresolved questions about the matrix. One major danger is to regard the matrix as a closed system, and to ignore the need to involve other groups within the education service itself. Head teachers and Principals, for example, can be regarded as a fourth dimension in the matrix, whose major contribution lies in implementing policies in the field, monitoring their effect and feeding back information to the centre.

A second major danger is to ignore the role of the Education Committee and its members. They relate directly to the Programme

Managers in their policy making role, and also to the Field Officers as watchdogs. They serve to bind the matrix even more firmly.

The third and most serious danger is of course to regard the education service as somethintg apart from local government. It maybe argued that the developments outlined in this paper illustrate the characteristic isolationism of the education service, and that in any case what is appropriate for a single service is of little help in devising schemes of corporate management for a local authority.

12. We would argue the contrary. In many respects an education service is a microcosm of the local authority as a whole, and its management problems are similar to those of the local authority. Some of its problems are noted below:

12.1 Size: the Sheffield education service spends over £30m a year and has 14,000 employees (1973/4).

12.2 Diffuseness: three hundred separate institutions.

12.3 Multipurpose: embraces meals, health, psychological, welfare and careers services.

12.4 Ill-defined aims: qualified manpower, individual fulfilment, good citizens, development of society.

12.5 Few measurable objectives.

12.6 No clear lines of accountability: DES and LEA, church and state, LEA and school, Education Committee and governors.

12.7 Internal departmentalism: Schools, Special Services, Further Education, Youth Employment, Adult, Youth.

Some of the difficulties mentioned arise from the nature of education or from the English educational system. In so far as the remainder can be solved by local systems and styles of management we believe the matrix will help us greatly. Above all the separation of the three main functions and the definition of many discrete but interlocking programme areas, are features of the matrix which would give vitality to the otherwise mechanistic management structures which seem likely to emerge in 1974.

The ultimate test is of course the quality of Sheffield education service.

We hope we have created the right sort of management structure for the creative problem solving role which an Education Department should fill.

(ii) Management by Objectives in Somerset Education Department

1. In 1969 elected members of the Somerset County Council were beginning to take an interest in new management techniques, and in particular in management by objectives. Subsequently this approach was introduced into the accountancy branch of the Treasurer's Department.

2. The interest of senior staff of the Education Department having been aroused at Local Government Training Board courses and not wishing to be out-distanced by our financial colleagues we accepted the invitation of the Management Services Committee to offer ourselves as a guinea pig to see if the techniques could be used effectively in a department such as Education.

3. We had made a clumsy and amateurish attempt ourselves at introducing this discipline but this had been ineffective and it was clear that, in the absence of anyone well-versed in this technique, outside consultants would be necessary. It was a condition that the Chief Education Officer should approve the choice of consultant and the need for this should be stressed. In fact we were fortunate in the choice and good relationships between members of the Department and the consultant were soon established.

4. H.M. Treasury's "Glossary of Management Techniques" has this to say about management by objectives —

    "a technique under which targets are fixed as a basis for achieving greater effectiveness throughout the whole of an organisation or part of an organisation.

    The system involves the fixing of agreed and realistic targets for an organisation (or part of it) in precise quantititive terms, e.g. to increase the output of work by x per cent, to reduce the time taken over a process by y per cent, or to reduce the error rate by z per cent. The factors which impede the attainment of these objectives are then identified and courses of action, including training, are agreed in order to remove them. The results achieved are periodically appraised and new targets set. It is important that individual targets are not only clear and realistic in themselves, but also that each should contribute effectively to the aims of the organisation. The approach is based on the view that targets agreed by a manager and his subordinates are in themselves an incentive and that they form a yardstick against which performance can be measured."

5. On this basis it might be thought that the technique is not applicable to a department such as Education. We could not, for example, arbitrarily decide to increase our output of educated people by 3% per annum. Nevertheless, we believe that eventually we arrived at a modified application of management by objectives which is useful in a department such as this.

6. The technique is set out in details elsewhere (1) but briefly, the modified system concerned itself with the objectives of the Department, the key areas in which these objectives can be achieved, the contribution of individual staff members in these key areas, measurement of performance, and the way in which the corporate work of the Department and the individual work of officers can be improved.

7. In searching for these modifications we spent a lot of time in somewhat philosophical — and with hind-sight, unnecessary — discussions on definitions. Education is a discipline which lends itself to pontification by those who enjoy the role of the philosopher king, and if one is not careful one spends hours pontificating but achieving nothing.

Objectives

8. We decided to distinguish between the objectives of the Education Committee and those of the Department and concentrate our energies on the latter. The Education Committee at that time had not in fact considered its objectives, and in discussing what was essentially management technique, we were concerned with the work of the Department and not the deliberations of the Committee. We deliberately tried to cast a dynamic role for the Department in considering what the teams as a whole were trying to do, as opposed to the more passive one of simply carrying out the instructions of the Education Committee. This latter role would have provided too ready an excuse for not achieving objectives on the grounds that the Committee had not agreed to the Department's proposals, whereas the preferred approach of considering the Department's role means that the lack of Committee approval to proposals must be regarded by the Department as a failure on their part: either they were wrong in identifying objectives which were unacceptable or, if the objectives were right, then the Department failed in the presentation of their case to the Committee.

9. We had, too, to take into account other restraints which might not have applied in industrial and commercial fields, particularly the professional rights of teachers in the matter of curriculum and the responsibilities of managers and governors of schools. Nevertheless, we did not wish to obscure our objectives by a series of qualifications and provisos referring to these restraints. No commanding General in a war, for example, would set as his objective "the seizure of hill 170 by 'X' division, subject to the availability of ammunition, the weakness of the enemy and the intervening river not being too wide for us to cross."

---

(1) "Management by Objectives in Local Government", Glendinning and Bullock, Charles Knight & Co. Ltd.

10. We therefore described our objectives very simply as being "to provide, maintain and improve the educational opportunities available to the people of Somerset".

Key Areas

11. The main areas are easily identifiable and follow the sequence of our objectives, i.e. the provision of new schools and colleges, their maintenance under the various heads of buildings, staff and equipment, and the improvement of opportunities including improved standards of service and curriculum reform. We perhaps strayed from the narrow path of simplicity and tended to analyse every activity of the senior management team rather than concentrating on the key areas which take up perhaps only 30% — 40% of anyone's time. However, from the point of view of a general review of the administration of the department and to make sure there were no gaps or overlapping, there was something to be said for this approach.

12. Taking the three-fold objectives of the Department — provision, maintenance and improvement — we then applied the approach to the work of the various branches — schools, further education, buildings and administration, the latter including finance, staffing and supplies.

Officers' Contributions

13. The essence of the approach was an analysis of the activities of each member of the senior management staff down to, and including, section heads. In fact it proved difficult at times to concentrate their attention on their activities because of an in-built tendency to waffle about responsibilities. At this point a fairly firm hand was needed either by the superior or by the consultant.

14. Each individual's work was described by himself as he saw it and then discussed with his immediate superior and his immediate subordinates. It was not surprising that in some cases several people claimed to be doing the same task. This reflected the confusion between overall responsibility and executive action. It proved a useful exercise and certainly led to greater delegation.

15. Eventually there was produced for all those concerned, what has since been described as a "manager's guide" showing for each key area his tasks, the level of performance to be achieved, the data needed to control and measure performance and a list of suggestions for improvements in performance in the coming year.

Measurement of Performance

16. The expected difficulties arose. How does one measure output and performance in education? Experience — certainly from the Victorian era onwards — shows that the system does not lend itself readily to measurement of output except in terms which distort the system because the measureable tends to drive out the

immeasurable. Since the memories of Victorian days with their emphasis on payment by results are so bitterly ingrained, the field was a sensitive one.

17. Our colleague from Messrs. Urwick Orr had come to us from a programme of advising a European government on stepping up pig production and — perhaps with his tongue in his cheek — he suggested we might measure our annual output of educated people.

18. Nevertheless, there are criteria for assessing the performance of individuals and teams within the Education Department, although these criteria do not always lend themselves readily to quantitative analysis and may be dismissed by some as being too subjective. Controls of the type concerned are —

The county's position in the education statistics published by the Society of County Treasurers.
Frequency of letters of complaint relating to any one matter and addressed personally to the chief education officer.
Newspaper reports and comment.
Feed-back from members of parliament, councillors, parents and managers, governors, heads, teachers' associations.
Reference back by committees for more information.
Overspending or underspending against estimates.

Improvements

19. Suggestions were invited for improving the performance of the Department and that of individuals. Here again we cast our net too wide and considered far too many suggestions. At the time in our enthusiasm this appeared not to matter but the full significance of this approach dawned when we came to the review stage which is described below.

20. Some of the improvements were really too trivial to have been recorded; some were of interest only to the particular individual and should not have found a place in a corporate document of this kind (for example, the manner in which one officer might choose to record the actions he had taken on a building project for his own information only). Among the welter of improvements there somehow slipped in the suggestion of a younger colleague that he should endeavour to get his salary increased. Nevertheless many of the improvements suggested were of undoubted value and the technique enabled us to assess the support among senior staff for some activities which had been decried by others (for example, the need to keep the schools development plan constantly up to date in the light of population changes). Some of the more useful improvements included:

The preparation by the Deputy Chief Education Officer of induction courses for newly-appointed senior staff.
The Assistant Education Officer for Buildings to introduce regular takeover inspections for all major projects with a feed-back on effectiveness.

The Research and Development Section to prepare network analysis charts for all secondary reorganisation schemes. (This one was prompted by the failure to issue public notices on schedule for one particular scheme).

Supplies section to report on maintenance and servicing of electronic and other technical equipment.

The Assistant Education Officer (Administration) to carry out a review of delegated powers to officers.

Encouragement to each school to produce an in-service training programme for its staff.

The mounting of a series of courses for school managers and governors on appointment procedures for staff.

The Chief Education Officer to see that the organisation and its operation are understood by all senior staff.

Follow-up

21. There was to be a follow-up procedure in November, six months after the scheme had been launched, and this follow-up was to involve a discussion of improvement plans and performance between each officer and his superior. It was at this stage that tensions and some impatience with the system became critical. The review period came at a time when senior members of the department were deeply involved in the political and public discussions of a major secondary reorganisation scheme, and there was a marked resentment from the Chief Education Officer downwards to devoting their time to discussion of this review. This reaction was aggravated when, in comparison with the other matters with which we should have been dealing, many of these so-called improvements stood exposed as the trivia they really were.

22. Nevertheless, this exercise focused attention on the extent to which senior education officers should be expected to involve themselves in improving the administrative machine when their efforts and energies were badly needed in their own educational field and here we detected a divergence of view between the management consultant and ourselves. I would suggest the separation of improvements into two groups —

22.1 those of direct reference to educational strategy or with policy implications which should involve the education officers, e.g. the preparation of a series of courses for managers and governors on appointing staff; and

22.2 improvements in the mechanism of administration, e.g. those connected with budget or contracting procedures, which might be dealt with by the senior administrative officer.

23. At this stage — and indeed increasingly through the exercise — we became conscious of the burden that must rest on the head of

the administrative element in an education department if the educationists are to be free to concentrate on the problems of education rather than those of adminsitration. Towards the end of the 1960's the chief administrative officer in the department was styled the Chief Clerk but by the time this exercise was put in hand his post had been re-designated as that of Assistant Education Officer for Administration. As a result of the exercise, it was further upgraded to that of a Senior Assistant Education Officer and in the organisation for the new Somerset one of the four Deputies, each responsible for a branch of the Department's work, is entitled Deputy Education Officer (Administration).

Suggestions for a Running Cycle

24. The process of management by objectives is undoubtedly a continuing one and can easily become a routine bore to which people respond as a rather unwanted imposition to be ignored if possible or got out of the way with the minimum of effort. If it is not to slip into this position the system has to be kept simple and seen clearly to be of value, whereas in our case the first run undoubtedly generated much too much paper and took up too much time.

25. As a continuing exercise something on the following lines might be advocated :

In February or March of each year action plans produced by each senior manager show how he will implement the developments and improvements envisaged in the Council's budget which will at that time of the year have been passed. Each action plan should be agreed by the immediate superior.

About June of each year further departmental branch and individual improvements can be discussed, particularly if the Council as a whole is at that time of the year starting to plan its development budget for the following year. At this stage too variations in individual responsibilities can be settled.

In the Autumn a review of the action plans and progress in implementing improvements and developments for the current year with the consequent amendment of the department's improvement programme for the following year should be undertaken, leading again to —

February or March the preparation of action plans for the coming year.

PART IV RESOURCE ALLOCATION AND MANAGEMENT

The education service ranges from nursery to higher education and includes small nursery schools, youth clubs and large polytechnics. Encompassed within the area of a single authority may be problems deriving from rural and urban, new estate or decaying housing, or advantaged and disadvantaged communities. In content and administration the service is therefore both diverse and dispersed. This presents within the education budget problems of allocation and management of resources. At the same time changes in the planning process and budgeting approach require a different flow of management information and may affect accountancy systems. Aspects of these problems are brought out in the following descriptions of developments in three authorities.

(i) The Primary School EPA Index and The Secondary School Index
— Inner London Education Authority

1. The ILEA Primary School EPA Index was an attempt to discriminate between primary schools on a new definition of education need. The impetus for the work came from the Plowden Report which spoke of areas where "educational handicaps are reinforced by social handicaps" and suggested that schools in such areas should benefit from "positive discrimination" in order "to raise schools with poor standards to the national average, and then quite deliberately to make them better".

2. The Plowden Report lists eight criteria for identifying EPAs:

Social class composition

Family size

Overcrowding and sharing of dwellings

Supplements in cash and kind from the state

Poor school attendance and truancy

Children unable to speak English

Retarded, disturbed, and handicapped pupils in schools

Incomplete families

The DES Circular 11/67 suggested two more:

Multiple deprivation because of the combination of several disadvantages in the environment

The general quality of the physical environment

Information on some of these factors was routinely collected by the Research and Statistics Group, other administrative branches held data on schools, the census provided information on the areas surrounding the schools. Other information could be gathered by surveys of the schools.

3. Initially in 1967 a pilot study was undertaken in two parts of the ILEA to see if it were possible to develop a scale with standard, reliable and reasonably accessible data. Subsequently data was collected for all ILEA primary schools and an index was constructed. Table 1 lists the criteria, measures and sources used to make up the index.

Table 1

Criterion	Measure	Source
(i) Social class composition	% males in unskilled and semi-skilled occupations	*1966 census
(ii) Large families	% children in households of 6 or more	*1966 census
(iii) Overcrowding	% households living at a density of more than $1\frac{1}{2}$ persons per room	*1966 census
(iv) Housing stress	% households without an inside W.C.	*1966 census
(v) Cash supplements	% pupils receiving free meals	1966 Sept. return
(vi) Absenteeism	% absent during 1st week in May	1967 May return
(vii) Immigrants	% immigrants in school	Form 7(i) 1967
(viii) Handicapped pupils	% pupils in bottom (lowest 25%) ability groups	1967 transfer
(ix) Teacher turnover	% teachers in school less than 3 years	1967 Teacher Record card
(x) Pupil turnover	% pupils who moved during year	1965/6 attendance card

*The catchment area (for which census information was derived) for each school was defined arbitrarily as a $\frac{1}{4}$ mile radius from the school, save for R.C. schools for which the distance was $\frac{1}{2}$ mile.

4. It was decided to weigh each of the criteria equally, and the school's score on each of the criteria was scaled thus:

$$Y = \begin{cases} \dfrac{x - (\bar{x} - 2S)}{4S} & \text{if } (\bar{x} - 2S) < x < (\bar{x} + 2S) \\ 0 & \text{if } x < (\bar{x} - 2S) \\ 100 & \text{if } x \geq (\bar{x} + 2S) \end{cases}$$

where x is the original score
$\bar{x}$ is the mean for all ILEA schools
S is the standard deviation of the original scores.

Thus the scale score in principle could go from 0 for the school(s) with the lowest percentage to 100 for the school with the highest. A school's final score on the index was the mean of the scale scores. In principle the final scores could also go from 0 to 100, in fact the range was rather less, from about 20 to 30. The schools were then ranked from 1 for the school with the highest score to 650 for the school with the lowest score. The higher the score the more deprived the school. The index has been recalculated twice since then, in 1970 and in 1974 with up to date information and on occasion new measures and new criteria. Pupil absenteeism was not found to discriminate efficiently between schools and was dropped in 1970, as was the criterion "housing stress as measured by the absence of an inside W.C." Two new criteria were included; parental lack of interest as measured by the percentage of parents not attending their child's first school medical examination and adequacy of the school building as measured by the number of children per 100 square feet of floor space. In place of Teacher Turnover a new measure of Teacher Stress, measured by the average number of short absences per teacher per school, was included. In the 1974 revision the criteria "Teacher Stress" was finally dropped, both because the measure failed to discriminate adequately between schools and more fundamentally because the critrion itself was felt to penalise schools working well in difficult circumstances. A new criterion "disturbed children" as measured by the percentage of fourth year Junior pupils with abnormally high scores on the Rutter child behaviour rating scale was included.

5. Criteria and measures will certainly be further revised in the future. Criteria chosen depend not only on what is thought to be important but also on what is thought to be politically acceptable. As Form 7(i) has now been withdrawn, the criterion "immigrants" will have to be dropped from the index.

6. The index does not define an EPA school nor does it measure any absolute level of deprivation; it ranks all ILEA primary schools in what is thought to be their order of "deprivation". Even if the criteria and measures had remained the same since the index was first produced a school's score and position on the index could change either because there had been an absolute change in the conditions in the school e.g. lower percentage of free meals, or because there had been a relative change, e.g. the same percentage of free meals in the school but a changed percentage within ILEA.

Use of the Index

7. The Authority has used the index in support of its claims to the DES for the primary school rebuilding programme and for extra payments to teachers in schools of special difficulty. Administratively it was, and is, used as the basis for the allocation of various kinds of additional resources and special help as between one school and another. In the first years of its use extra help and resources were given to schools ranking above a certain position on the index. This method of allocation was not only an unfortunate kind of poverty trap but had the further disadvantage that statistically there might only be a difference in the fourth decimal place in the score of the school that received extra help and the school that did not. To overcome this a new scheme (the alternative use of resources) was introduced by which half the total additional resources were, and are, distributed pro rata to roll weighted by the EPA index score.

The Secondary School Index

8. The Schools Sub-Committee of ILEA had decided that resources should be allocated to secondary schools according to need. It was necessary therefore that the secondary school index should be broadened in scope more than the primary school EPA index. Needs in this context were considered to be characteristics of the school over which the school has virtually no control and which make the problem of teaching more or less difficult. Those aspects of the school that are a reflection of the efficiency of the school should not be included. Were such items included teachers would rightly consider that the more effectively they carried out their job the less resources they, and their school, would receive from the Authority.

9. Table 2 lists the criteria, measures and sources used in the secondary school index.

Table 2

Criterion	Measure	Sources
(a) **Children's Social and Intellectual Background**		
Backward children	% of 11+ pupils in the lowest ability band	Secondary School Admissions
Immigrants	% immigrants in the school	Form 7(i)
Poverty	% of pupils in attendance receiving free meals	School return
Large families	% of children in families of 4 or more children	Literacy Survey
One parent families	% of pupils not living with both natural parents	Literacy Survey
Social class	% of pupils with semi-skilled/unskilled guardians	Literacy Survey
Pupil turnover	% of pupils who changed schools	Special return
(b) **School Buildings**		
Adequacy of Buildings	Split site (main class-bases only)	Education Officer's Records
	Floor space/ child	Ditto
	Site area/child	Ditto
	Age of building (pre or post 1903)	Ditto
	Tall buildings (lift)	Ditto

(c) **Special Factors**

| Technical Studies | % of teaching staff who are handicraft/ housecraft/technical teachers | Special return from from DOs |

10. The scores were scaled in the same way as in the primary school index. However, the factors were not weighted equally. Within the first factor the measures of the children's background were weighted equally. Within the second factor, school buildings, the measures were weighted in the ratio 3:3:3:1:1. The three broad factors were weighted in the ratio 6:2:1. These weightings were justified in the light of experience and judgement of the relative importance of these considerations in school administration. When it was agreed to construct the index in 1972 it was realised that disturbed children were presenting serious problems to schools. At the time there was no agreement on suitable school based data. Since then agreement has been reached on a suitable measure and the criterion has been included in the primary EPA index, and will be included in the next revision of the secondary school index.

11. As in the primary school index, the inclusion of criteria is dependent on the availability of suitable data. Immigrants will therefore have to be dropped as a criterion.

12. An alternative use of resources scheme like the scheme for primary schools was introduced for secondary schools in September, 1973 and the secondary school index plays the same role as the primary school index.

Discussion

13. In providing extra resources for schools in particularly difficult situations care has to be taken to ensure that the extra resources are not given, or thought to be given, to schools that are inefficient. In so far as their pupils' behaviour or attainment on verbal reasoning tests is influenced by the school, it is clearly desirable that these measures should be taken at the beginning of the child's primary or secondary school rather than the end.

(ii) Alternative Use of Resources Scheme — Inner London Education Authority

1. The Alternative Use of Resources (AUR) Scheme was introduced by the Inner London Education Authority in its primary schools in September, 1972 and in its secondary schools in September, 1973. Its main aims are threefold: first to enable schools to play a major role in determining for themselves how best to deploy the resources placed at their disposal and to involve teachers together with heads in the process of decision making; second to provide the opportunity for schools to plan ahead the ways in which their major resources may be allocated to achieve particular developments within the school's organisation and curriculum; and third to enable the Authority to exercise positive discrimination between schools according to their special needs.

2. As a by-product the scheme has also brought about considerable simplification of the basis and methods of resource allocation. This has been achieved by ceasing to use the weighted roll and instead basing staffing allowances and the allocation of other resources on simple estimated rolls. The school allowance is now made for the academic year to bring it into line with the other resources which are already made on this basis. School allowances are also calculated as a flat rate per pupil rather than on a per capita basis with varying rates for different ages and allowances for certain specialist activities and accommodation. Moreover schools are able to carry forward balances from one academic year to the next. Finally, where vacancies in teaching or non-teaching staff arise, either in basic staff or in additional positions for which the school has opted, the unused resources can, within prescribed limits, be redeployed (redeployment of this type involving a positive decision on the part of the school not to fill the vacancy for the period in question).

3. Before dealing with the basic mechanics of the Scheme it may be helpful to mention the two familiar means of allocating non-capital resources that have commonly been employed hitherto.

3.1 The traditional method is for the local authority to distribute a sum of resources parcelled up under a number of headings and to require expenditure to take place only within those headings. Resources may not be transferred from one heading to another and money left unspent in one financial year cannot be carried over into the next. The resources allocated by the local authority may or may not be related, either in amount or kind, to the needs of that individual school as distinct from a type of school or its size. This system assumes that "the local authority knows best" and does little to encourage responsibility or flexibility in the ways in which schools use their resources.

3.2 More recently the method known as virement has become familiar. The study group on the Government of Colleges of

Education (the Weaver Committee) defined virement as "power to switch money from one head of estimates to another". A particular benefit of virement is that it enables resource-allocation to follow more closely upon changes in needs and priorities which were unseen at the stage when the estimates were approved.

Inner London secondary schools have been able to exercise a measure of virement since September, 1970 when they were enabled to reallocate up to 5% of their total resources, although not all schools wished to do so. The Weaver Committee recommended that colleges should have power to allocate money within each of certain broad heads of estimates separately but not between these broad groups.

4. The Alternative Use of Resources Scheme' however adopts a different approach by distinguishing between resources which can be used in whatever way is desired and certain basic minimum entitlements at the same time. The resources include elements based solely upon the school roll and others allocated according to differing needs. It can best be understood by examining the main categories of resources available to each school as set out in the following table.

	Basic provision according to roll	Discretionary provision according to special needs
Schools cannot reallocate	Basic teaching staff Basic non-teaching staff	Full-time teaching staff and non-teaching staff for immigrants and special needs
Schools can reallocate	School allowance	Additional resources

5. To deal now with each of these in turn:

5.1 **Teaching Staff**

The basic entitlement is determined according to the Authority's current policy (governed of course by the national supply of teachers and the Department's quota). This is reviewed annually and is now expressed in terms of pupil/teacher ratio to be applied to an estimate of the school's roll for the year concerned. For the 1974/5 school year this will be 1 :29 for primary schools and 1 :17 for secondary schools. In order to achieve these standards, it will still be necessary for a small margin of 'off quota' teachers to be included in the secondary schools' basic (1 :17) provision although the whole of the basic for primary schools will be 'on-quota'. In addition some schools will receive an extra specific allocation for help with immigrant pupils and since these teachers come from a special allowance made for this purpose by the Department of Education and Science over the ILEA 'quota' they too must be included in the school's minimum complement which cannot be reallocated.

Provlsion for extra teaching help is then in the separate allocation of "additional resources" referred to below.

5.2 **Non-teaching staff**

Just as for teachers, the Authority sets a minimum provision for nursery assistants, women helpers and part-time secretaries in primary schools and technicians, librarians, office staff, media resources officers etc., in secondary schools. The basic allocation is set against the same roll estimates. Basic entitlements similarly will include an element for high immigrant numbers as well. Here again an extra discretionary allowance will be included by the Divisional Officer in the 'additional resources' sum according to special needs.

5.3 **School Allowance**

Apart from the provision for school equipment, books and consumable materials, this sum embraces what used to be known as the 'activities and amenities' allowance to finance such things as educational visits, transport to sporting activities etc. By the same token it is this 'pocket' which schools wishing to make extra provision for special activities and visits must supplement as necessary.

The basic allocation by the Authority to primary schools is a straightforward per capita sum applied to the estimated rolls plus a lump sum. (For 1974/5 the allowances for primary schools will be a per capita sum of £5.20 plus lump sums as follows : Nursery class £34 : Nursery school £150 : Infant school £225 : Junior school £375 : J.M. & I. school £325. For secondary schools there will be a per capita sum of £14 per boy and £15 per girl.

5.4 **Additional Resources**

The sum allocated under this heading, together with the school allowance is the money available to heads for reallocation. In considering his recommendations for apportioning the additional resources money between his schools, the District Inspector will have regard to any additional staff a school may require above the basic standards and will try to ensure that each school has available a reasonable proportion of extra money for such things as activities, projects, curricular development, etc. For this purpose he will look to the relative positions of schools on the Authority's index of educational priority as well as draw upon his personal knowledge of schools' particular problems.

6. It is, I think, worth mentioning here that in working on the latest practicable estimates of school rolls and attempting to give schools as much time as possible to decide upon their allocations, there is little time available for the complex administrative procedures involved in the scheme. It is therefore particularly important that each stage is completed in the period allotted in the timetable. Schools are notified in February of the total amounts of resources allocated for the following academic year. Heads then decide after consultation with staffs according to the internal management arrangements within the schools, how they wish to deploy the total resources available for reallocation. These decisions are set out on a form provided for the purpose and sent to the Divisional Officer early in the Summer Term. The decisions are then reported to school governing bodies later in the term.

7. The options open to a school are therefore the ways to redeploy the money available for reallocation between the various types of staffing, the allowances for equipment and activities and, to a small extent, minor building works. For the purposes of the Scheme, a fixed value is placed upon each type of teaching and non-teaching staff (full-time or part-time) based, where necessary, upon an average of current scales and heads are notified of these so that they can make precise allocations without having to be concerned with the actual salaries of individuals. As already stated, balances may be carried forward from one academic year to the next. (With regard to minor building works, although the Government exercises strict control over the expenditure by LEA's on building work each year, the Authority has been given a concession by the Department of Education and Science which enables county schools to use their allowances under the AUR scheme to finance small improvement jobs costing up to a limit of £1,250 each. At a time of particular stringency because of cuts in the ILEA's minor works allocation, many schools have welcomed this opportunity to get such long awaited jobs done as the installation of sinks, provision of display boarding or enlargement of storage facilities etc. Any one job contemplated must be kept within the cost limit and, in order to ensure that the money will actually be spent in the year concerned, the order to have work carried out must be issued by the end of November).

8. To show more clearly how the head carries out his function of exercising choice, examples are given below of the way in which the allowances are presented on each school's allocation form (left-hand side) and how (on the right of the same form) a head might choose to redistribute that part of his allowances available for reallocation.

63

Primary School
(Roll 320+40 part-time Nursery)

1. Basic full-time teaching
   staff (excluding head) 11
   Nursery teachers 1
   Additional for other needs 1
2. Teaching staff for
   immigrants 3
3. Basic non-teaching staff:
   Nursery Assistants 1
   Women helpers (weekly
   hrs.) $32\frac{1}{2}$
   Secretarial (weekly hrs.) 26

4. Resources available for £
   reallocation
   School allowance 2,055
   Additional resources 5,520

   7,575

Secondary School
(Roll 1,220)

1. Basic teaching staff (1:17
   including head)

   On-quota 64
   Off-quota 7.8
2. Teaching staff for
   immigrants 3
3. Basic non-teaching staff
   Secretary 1
   Clerical/Typist
   full-time 2
   part-time (hours) $37\frac{1}{2}$
   General Assistant (hours) 25

   Librarian 1
   Media Resources Officer 1
   Technicians 7.5
   Storekeeper —
4. General Assistants for
   immigrants $12\frac{1}{2}$
5. Resources available for
   reallocation
   School allowance 18,300
   Additional Resources 11,575

   29,875

Head's proposed allocations (of item 4)	No. of staff	Values £
Teaching staff		
Part-time qualified	.5	1,000
Instructors & pre-college students		—
Music teachers		—
Non-teaching staff		
Nursery Assistants		—
Women helpers	80 hrs.	2,000
Additional meals supervisors		—
Secretarial	3 hrs.	105
School allowance		4,370
Minor works		100
		7,575

Head's proposed allocations (of item 5)	No. of staff	Values £
Teaching staff		
Part-time qualified	1.5	3,500
Instructors and pre-college students		—
Music teachers	5	500
Non-teaching staff		
Clerical/Typist		—
General Assistant	1	1,200
Additional meals supervisors		—
Librarian		—
Media Resources Officer		—
Technicians	1	1,900
Storekeeper		—
Others		—
		£
School allowance		21,275
Minor works		1,500
		29,875

9. These are, of course, purely notional examples and might not be realised in any particular school. Reduction of these resources to a cash denominator means that the resource "input" can be directly compared. As an example of the kind of managerial decision to which this scheme leads, a school might be imagined in which a choice was being made between providing 10 teaching sets in Maths to cover a total of eight classes in the second and third forms, and employing an extra half librarian. The former would involve .75 of a teacher, at a "cost" of £1,500: the latter would cost £1,250 (these are average, notional figures). One group of staff no doubt favours the use of resources in the one way; another urges the value of the librarian. (In point of fact the cost of setting in Maths is appreciably greater than the cost of the extra half-time librarian). As things are commonly arranged, that decision would not be made by the school. It would either get or not get enough staff to have 10 sets for the teaching of Maths; it would either get or not get the extra half-time librarian in relation to the size of the school. If, however, both of these advances lie within the scope of resources over and above the basic minimum, then the decision can effectively be taken in the place where it should be taken — namely, the school itself, which must judge its own priorities in relation to its total curricular needs.

10. It is perhaps worth mentioning some of the demands which the scheme will make upon the school itself. It is essential that heads should make decisions about resources reallocations in full consultation with staff. Real opportunities will thus arise for staff to become involved in managerial decisions. If staff are not involved, the resulting decisions may be neither wise nor acceptable. Heads will hence be concerned in a major administrative task: the organisation of effective participation. The corollary of giving the school itself greater responsibility in resource allocation should therefore be to increase the responsibility of the teacher in the organisation of the learning process. Moreover the terms of the scheme, and especially the facility to carry unspent resources over into the subsequent academic year, will both encourage and require planning on the school's part, whilst helping to promote and clarify discussion of the school's objectives. Finally, the scheme may enable administrators and inspectors and all those not actually in schools on a day-to-day basis to perceive more clearly what teachers think their schools' needs really are.

(iii) Greater London Council/Inner London Education Authority Management Accounting System

1. Introduction

1.1 Management Accounting was introduced in 1969 in the Greater London Council and the Inner London Education Authority. This was designed to enable members and management at all levels to monitor performance regularly against intended activity as expressed in the annual budget.

1.2 The Planning-Programming-Budgeting System was then in its infancy and although the GLC (not in this case the Inner London Education Authority) were studying the case for it, the Management Accounting scheme was conceived long before. It seemed reasonable to undertake the next review with a revised scheme to operate from the date (April 1973) on which it was planned to go "live" on the Planning-Programming-Budgeting System. The scheme finally adopted can deal with a variety of management structures; indeed it effectively meets the requirements of the Inner London Education Authority even though the latter did not introduce the PPB system. And if the Council or Authority decide to alter their management system the basic elements of the present Management Accounting Scheme would still be adequate.

1.3 In planning and in controlling, managers are concerned with defining the needs of the community and achieving the goals intended to meet these needs. An investigation into the requirements of every department of the Council and ILEA and the design of the scheme took just over a year and the final specification was produced in December 1971, leaving one and a quarter years for computer programming.

1.4 Management accounting must cover budgetary control, financial accounting and in some areas cost accounting. It must also seek to link up with the achievement of objectives in physical terms; this is very much more difficult to define and quantify.

1.5 In devising the scheme in 1969 the basic principles of accounting were considered afresh. Although the practice of receipts and payments accounting has its attractions — mainly of simplicity — it was decided that income and expenditure accounting with the additional facilities for the entering of commitments and liabilities would give better control because the first and essential point for financial control is before an order is placed. Full-scale commitment accounting has not yet been achieved because the extra cost and the extra human effort cannot yet be justified.

1.6 The new scheme demands considerable effort and active co-operation from many people at many levels of management in all departments. One of the keys to success lies in the effectiveness of the "crosswalks" between (a) knowing and controlling the total costs of (i.e. the money value of the resources devoted to) the specific programmes, objectives and activities that make up the Programme Budget, and (b) knowing and controlling the cost of the individual and separate types of resource (staff, materials, land and buildings) which contribute towards achieving those programmes. In this exercise the allocation of the cost of the many staff who are concerned with a number of different programmes and activities is a difficult task, but it is an important and significant one if staff are to be used to fullest advantage.

2. Different categories of management

The Council's management structure responsible for achieving its goals can be conveniently grouped under the headings of:

2.1 Corporate management of the authority as a whole, responsible for the review of overall functions, policies, allocation of resources and review of achievement.

Within the GLC the Policy and Resources Committee has overall responsibility to the Council for assessing objectives for the Council's services and the allocation of resources. The Director-General's Board of Chief Officers provides the principal forum for this corporate management at officer level.

2.2 Programme management, involved in the arrangements for assessing and meeting the needs of the community within a specific programme area. The Executive Committees of the Council are responsible for the management of their programmes. At officer level, Programme Boards comprising senior officers of the departments involved in a specific programme area are responsible for all the activities in that area; they will assist the Committees to formulate plans to give effect to the Council's policies, to supervise the analysis of specific policies and the alternative ways of implementing these policies, to monitor physical and financial progress and ensure the effective and efficient implementation of approved programmes.

2.3 Departmental management, responsible to programme management for carrying out the activities of specific programmes and also for the efficient provision of services, sometimes of a specialist nature, e.g. professional and trading departments.

2.4 Resource management, for planning, review and use of particular resources by the entire GLC organisation, e.g. land, manpower, finance.

3. Planning and Control

3.1 Planning

The Council's policies are set out in a multi-year plan (the next ensuing budget year together with, very broadly and approximately, the resource implications of current policies over the following four years). This provides an indication of the Council's objectives in the short and long term, quantified in financial terms and as far as practicable in terms of physical output and impact on the community. Objectives with associated costs are specified in greater detail in the budget year and identified with individual budget centres in departments. The management accounting system provides a supporting budgetary information system to assist management in the successful attainment of their objectives.

3.2 Control

In this context budgetary control covers, in outline —

3.2.1 the preparation of budgets relating the responsibilities of budget centres within departments to the requirements of programme plans; at higher levels this concept applies between Programme Committees and a Programme Board;

3.2.2 the regular comparison of actual expenditure with budgeted expenditure; thus contributing data for consideration of questions such as (i) Has the work been completed? (ii) Did we get value for money? (iii) Was the alterations and improvements programme for which a budget was provided, completed and to the specified standards?

Management is thereby in a much stronger position to —

3.2.3 take action where necessary to ensure that the budget outputs are achieved or revised;

3.2.4 ascertain trends which would involve amendments to objectives in the multi-year plan;

3.2.5 make adjustments to resource use to retain expenditure within the budget. It may be necessary to consider seeking authority for virement and/or supplements to the budget provisions.

4. Objectives of the Management Accounting Scheme

4.1 the principal objective of the management accounting scheme is 'to gather, process, present and interpret accounting information, financial and non-financial, that will assist management in the formulation of policy and the control of day to day operations of the Council/ILEA'. It must provide a supporting service to the differing levels and types of management involved in translating goals and objectives into work programmes and the subsequent monitoring of achievement. This requires that —

4.1.1 the information provided must meet the decision-making needs of the recipient and contain only the amount of detail applicable to his responsibilities;

4.1.2 estimates must be correctly apportioned to match the expected incidence of expenditure over the financial year: departmental budget centres are able to use a two-character code to indicate the expected incidence of expenditure for particular estimates;

4.1.3 actual expenditure must be readily and correctly coded, recorded and analysed: the coding of input into the accounting scheme is mainly undertaken by officers in spending departments;

4.1.4 the accounting returns to budget centres show the extent to which a given authorisation for expenditure has been used, whether by payments or by commitments and liabilities incurred: they indicate the variances of under-or over-spending during the period under review;

4.1.5 all reports must be adequate, timely, pertinent, concise and easily understood by the recipient: maximum use is to be made of reports providing only significant variances (exceptions) from budget: the frequency of reporting must be geared to the needs of the individual budget centres;

4.1.6 where practicable relevant non-financial information is considered together with the accounting returns prepared by the Treasurer: in many instances it is convenient for the departmental finance officer to annotate the accounting returns with the required supplementary information;

4.1.7 the accounting returns should show, in addition to the record of payments in summary form, the total of most commitments for future expenditure (covering orders and contracts placed) and for liabilities for goods and services received for which payment has not been made;

4.1.8 significant departures from the expected level of expenditure are brought to the attention of the departmental finance officer as well as to the budget centre in the department concerned.

5. The nature of the Management Accounting output

5.1 The financial information requirements of management are largely met by monthly returns processed by computer. The information is derived from the coding of expenditure and income according to the activities carried out and to the budget centres concerned. This use of coding enables returns to be prepared for the appropriate manager on either a programme or departmental basis. Additional information is held within the computer for each activity as to the responsible Committee and the relationship of that activity to the higher levels contained in each programme group structure. Diagrams 3, 4 and 5 give an outline of the Scheme, of the Accounting Code Structure, and of Departmental "Budget Centre" Returns.

5.2 Where required, the accounting returns presented to budget centres indentify the costs relating to individual premises, jobs, processes, etc. This information is obtained by extended use of the coding on invoices and other input, thus providing integrated accounting-costing.

5.3 Programme Committees, the Director-General's Board of Chief Officers and the Programme Boards of Senior Officers do not receive computer produced returns directly. The information presented at these levels is prepared individually from returns provided to departmental management.

5.4 The emphasis on departmental accounting needs has led to many different uses of the accounting code structure (as would be expected in view of the wide range of work undertaken throughout the Council and the ILEA). Departments are asked to use certain standard codings to enable information to be analysed and collated for Committees but are able to determine a substantial range of supplementary analyses for their own purposes by using other sections of the code structure.

6. Coding

6.1 The output from the management accounting scheme is intended to assist management and the subsequent action taken on the information provided forms the *raison d'etre* of the scheme. Managers must be able to rely on the information provided in the returns as to particular areas requiring attention; correct coding is therefore of the utmost importance. Staff engaged in the coding of data must have a clear knowledge of the code structure. The correct use of the accounting code is essential since incorrect input must mean misleading output.

6.2 Having regard to the various management levels and responsibilities, an accounting code structure of twenty characters has been devised to meet the management accounting requirements of all departments, including those of Education. The first seven give a broad objective/subjective analysis of expenditure and income. The other 13 give detailed returns under premises and managers and for costing. Not all these 13 are used by everyone. A considerable degree of ingenuity has been necessary to keep the number of characters to no more than twenty, but the greater the number the greater the possibility of error.

DIAGRAM 3 OUTLINE OF THE MANAGEMENT ACCOUNTING SCHEME

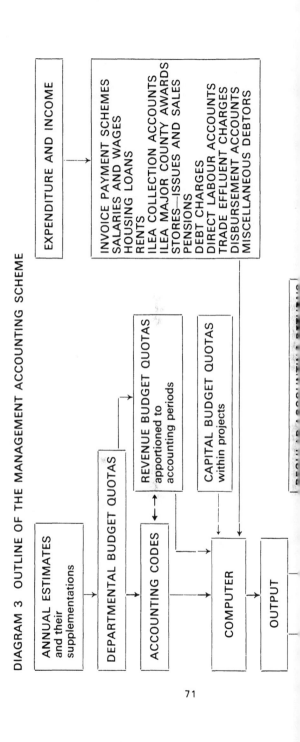

NOTES TO DIAGRAM 3

1. Following the approval by the Council of the estimates for the budget year the amounts (quotas) relating to each departmental budget centre are fed into the computer. Subsequent variations of these estimates are also processed amending the original figures stored within the computer.

2. An accounting code is attached to each budget quota; this enables the quota to be stored and retrieved in the variety of analyses required by the spending department and/or the department responsible for the PPB Activity/ILEA Service.

3. By the use of a two character indicator against each budget quota, departments are able to apportion the estimate over the monthly accounting periods to match the expected incidence of expenditure.

4. Expenditure and income is recorded within the computer by two basic methods:

4.1 from some two dozen related computer schemes giving information about chargeability processed through those schemes, e.g. salaries, invoice payments schemes, direct labour accounts;

4.2 by the use of specially designed schedules from departments giving the information on individual transactions.

5. Expenditure includes, when merited, sums for commitments in respect of goods/services ordered but not received together with sums for liabilities arising from goods/services received but not paid for.

6. The above information is analysed to produce regular accounting returns presented to varying levels of management within agreed formats at the frequency requested by the department(s) responsible.

DIAGRAM 4 ACCOUNTING CODE STRUCTURE

The revenue and capital code structures are set against the twenty character accounting code as shown below. The terms used include 'budget centre' and 'cost centre'; their meanings within the accounting scheme are:—

1. a budget centre means a section, location, branch or other division within a department for which (i) a separate budget is prepared and (ii) accounting returns are to be supplied on a regular basis;

2. a cost centre is regarded as the smallest accounting unit for which costs will be collected and could be, for example, a location, building, process, function and so on.

REVENUE CODE STRUCTURE 1		ACCOUNTING CODE POSITIONS 2	CAPITAL CODE STRUCTURE 3
DESCRIPTIONS			DESCRIPTIONS
Programme Group		1	
Activity		2 3	Project Number
Type of Expenditure (Subjective Analysis)	Group Sub-Groups Detail Sub-Detail	4 5 6 7	Type of Expenditure
Spending Department		8	Spending Department
Departmental Costing (Budget and Cost Centres)		9 10 11	Budget Centre
		12 13 14	Budget Centre Costing
Programme Costing		15 16 17	Project Costing
		18 19 20	

DIAGRAM 5   OUTPUT — BUDGET CENTRE RETURNS (REVENUE)

ACCOUNTING CODE ANALYSIS PRODUCES RETURNS BY

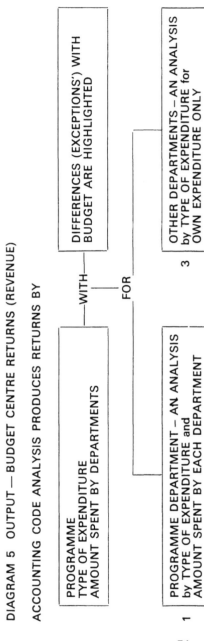

PROGRAMME
TYPE OF EXPENDITURE
AMOUNT SPENT BY DEPARTMENTS

———WITH———

DIFFERENCES (EXCEPTIONS') WITH
BUDGET ARE HIGHLIGHTED

———FOR———

1   PROGRAMME DEPARTMENT — AN ANALYSIS
by TYPE OF EXPENDITURE and
AMOUNT SPENT BY EACH DEPARTMENT

3   OTHER DEPARTMENTS — AN ANALYSIS
by TYPE OF EXPENDITURE for
OWN EXPENDITURE ONLY

BUDGET CENTRES ALSO RECEIVE, WHERE APPLICABLE, RETURNS FOR

NOTES TO DIAGRAM 5

The diagram outlines the principal types of accounting returns issued to budget centres within departments.

The four major returns meet the specific requirements of management as follows :—

1. Programme ('lead') department

    Details are supplied monthly in summary form, rather than at invoice level, of expenditure (and income) incurred by each department on programmes for which the programme department has a 'lead' role. The expenditure is set against the budget estimate as apportioned over the financial year to the date of the return and to the annual budget. Comments are added drawing the attention of managers to variances, within agreed parameters, between expenditure including commitments and liabilities and the budget apportionment and/or, the annual budget.

2. Other departments

    Similar information is presented monthly to each department, other than the programme department; details are however restricted to the spending department's own budgets and expenditure.

3. Programme Costing

    A lead department will wish to obtain the costs of specific items within a programme and appropriate use of the accounting code enables the records to be maintained and the information subsequently obtained. Requirements vary from department to department, e.g. the Education Department will identify the costs of special boarding schools, the Housing Department requires costs related to types or ages of dwellings and the Director of Establishments seeks a breakdown of training costs.

4. Budget Centres

    Each spending department is able to identify its budget centres within the accounting code and thereby receive returns covering the activities of each centre. In addition the code allows for each budget to obtain details of its costings, e.g. the separate costs of individual jobs undertaken by the centre.

(iv) Resource Allocation in Somerset

1. This is an odd time in which to write of the allocation of resources. Nevertheless, in the hope that soon we shall once again be able to give systematic thought to the subject, this paper describes the system built up in Somerset over the past few years.

2. Previously the budgeting system was of the more traditional pattern, with Committees putting up their own capital programmes and preparing their own revenue estimates; the Finance Committee, when it attempted to limit rate increases, would recommend amendments to Committees' estimates (the amendments were not always those which spending committees might themselves have suggested); and finally at the Council meeting it was open to any member to move the deletion of any item of which he disapproved. It was thus not uncommon for a fairly important item, especially if it marked a new development, to be rejected, while less deserving items, often obscured under general headings, went unchallenged.

3. The new system evolved gradually, and at first different departments had different approaches. Common to all was a basis of:

   Capital Budget
   Continuation Budget
   Development Budget
   Manpower Budget
   Capital Budget

4. This speaks for itself, but the technique is still evolving. A list of key-sector projects approved by the government departments has generally been the basis of the budget, together with approved non-key sector projects.

5. More recently — and independent of the current crisis — this approach was leading to difficulties. The government departments apparently work with some independence and we reached a stage when the Council was faced in one year with:

   a substantial "basic needs" programme for schools;
   a substantial programme for primary school replacement;
   a new tertiary college;
   a larger programme for the Social Services Committee;
   a network of health clinics,
   a heavy programme of road improvements, partly influenced
     by the extension of the M5 into Somerset,
   together with a considerable programme of non-key sector
     projects.

6. This embarrassing avalanche of permissions to spend money prompted the Council to require a forward costing of the revenue implications of these programmes. Perhaps not surprisingly the totals showed revenue increases beyond the limits which the Government had indicated.

7. The current crisis at least settled this difficulty; but basically the problem remains — i.e. the co-ordination of heavy programmes agreed by Ministries in the area of any one authority. If the Authority itself exercises restraint, it follows that in one field or another it may get out of step with government policies.

8. Continuation Budget
This was the basis of financial planning. The Continuation Budget was projected forward at constant prices and updated for price increases at the November preceding the year of estimate.

8.1 the cost of existing services at existing volumes and standards;

8.2 the cost of bringing into use capital projects already approved by the Council;

8.3 additional costs for growth of population at existing standards.

9. This budget was prepared by the officers and it was generally understood that it was not the subject of debate — although agreement clearly had to be reached between the financial officers and the spending departments on "growth". An increase in the school population of compulsory school age was clearly a growth requiring resources at a defined level; the growth of VIth forms was also accepted — perhaps with less justification.

10. More difficult was further education growth — here a percentage increase was agreed largely on a basis of guesswork with regard to past patterns and the size of the relevant Vth form population (for Technical College admission) and of the 18-year-old population for awards. We cannot claim success in this field — e.g. we financed 1973/74 on the basis of 15% growth in student hours in FE colleges but achieved only 3%. At the same time we budgeted for 1330 new major FE awards but made only 1160.

11. This allocation of resources meant that other branches of education had been unnecessarily deprived; moreover, extra FE staff having been appointed, it is difficult to get back to the previous staffing ratios.

12. The problem remains — how satisfactorily to relate in-put and out-put in FE, bearing in mind the element of independence granted to governors under their Articles of Government.

13. To a lesser degree there was the question of growth in other elements of education, e.g. the youth service and special education. That it was no great problem reflected the reasonable attitude of our financial colleagues.

14. It is important to realise that this forward budgeting was on the basis of fixed prices. The Education Committee, with one important exception, did not have to budget for future inflation — this was the responsibility of the Finance Committee who set aside a substantial contingency fund to cover supplementary estimates from spending departments for pay and price increases as the year went by.

15. The exception concerned the capitation allowances for schools. These were notified at the beginning of the financial year and remained fixed for that period, whether prices rose or not. It is historically uncertain whether the annual increase reflected price increases in retrospect or in advance — in an era of steady inflation the problem was really academic. But more recently the graph of price increases has taken on an exponential appearance which would have raised the issue this year — had not current restrictions settled the matter beyond question!

16. The continuation budgets of the spending committees were then totalled, subtracted from the resources available, and the balance was regarded as available for developments.

17. This perhaps over-simplifies the issue — how to calculate the resources available. It was not sufficient to assess the rate increase that was likely to be acceptable (but even this could arouse arguments of political philosophy); there had also to be some idea of the level of government grants.

18. The Council instead tended to take as a basis for its forward planning the projections for each service published in the Government's annual White Papers on Public Expenditure. These gave in broad terms some idea of the growth rate for the various elements of the education service, to which should be added an agreed element to represent the extent to which the population growth in the County justified an excess allowance over the national figure.

19. The weakness in this system is obvious. The White Paper can deal only in broad terms, and its authors are too remote from the root of things for their estimates, taken one heading at a time, to have the degree of accurancy needed as a basis for committee estimates.

20. For example, the amount approved for the development budget for 1973/74 was 0.9% of the Committee's estimated net expenditure, after allowing for the growth forecast in the White Paper. An error of $\frac{1}{2}$% in the latter figure could have had the effect of halving the development budget.

21. One cannot be satisfied, too, with a system in which spending committees are debarred from putting in hand what they regard as important developments, in order to keep the budget within prescribed limits, when the outcome is for the county balance at the end of the year to be very substantially greater than estimated.

22. More recently the Government has tried to exercise control over the rate increase. Here arbitrary figures have been used irrespective of the varying circumstances in each county, and which apparently ignore the increased revenue costs of the programmes, especially capital programmes, approved by the various Ministries.

The Development Budget

23. The Council having decided what sum could be allocated for development, the various Committees were asked for their pro-

posals — but oddly enough it was not accepted that a committee could argue for the full growth indicated for its service in the White Paper. On the contrary, it was claimed that the Council had the right to settle its own priorities within services, whatever the Government's priorities might be.

24. The Education Committee annually reviewed its main targets, and projected these four years ahead in terms of money and manpower — here again using Government White Papers, including Mrs. Thatcher's ill-starred "Framework for Expansion". Consequently our requirements were ready at hand.

25. It is not to be wondered at that the total requirements of the committees exceeded the sum set aside by the Council. In one year the Policy Advisory Committee were moved to recommend the Council to make more money available; but generally that Committee had the invidious task of choosing between the well-argued claims of the spending committees, most of them quoting policy statements from their respective Ministries in their support.

26. The advent of Corporate Management gave the elected members a welcome way out — the Chief Officers' Committee would advise on the reductions that should be made to keep the development budgets down to the required level!

27. There followed a curious sequence. It so happened that the Education list was the first to be considered. We had asked for £350,000 of developments (excluding capital projects) and realising something had to be done, we offered to reduce this to £300,000 — for which we had no authority whatsoever from the Education Committee.

28. Finally the Chief Officers were able to report reductions of the required amount to the Policy Committee, where (and at the subsequent Finance and Council meetings) one had the picture of elected members arguing — not without success — for the restoration of the cuts which the officers had made.

29. Some colleagues at this stage pleaded for something similar to the cabinet tradition of support for cabinet decisions; others argued that if a professional chief officer genuinely believed that his service would suffer as the result of decisions made by the Chief Officers Committee, he had a duty to advise his Chairman, and indeed his full Committee, to oppose the Chief Officers' recommendations.

30. There may be a tendency for a Policy Committee to stick by their Chief Officers reductions in resisting changes. To accept one restoration must mean finding a corresponding reduction and re-opening the whole issue — unless the Council is asked to vote more money or the balances are raided.

31. An exception to this rule will arise if there is a marked divergence of view between Chief Officers and the members — this could easily happen in a service (police for example) which is dear to the hearts of senior and influential members, but which is looked upon more critically by the Chief Officers.

32. Now this may reflect good management, but it can be the negation of local government. Responsibilities can be left to the officers which should be taken by the members; and at key stages the chairmen of the major committees can find themselves excluded from the bargaining — on the grounds that they would merely support each other's proposals.

The Manpower Budget

33. This is an important management tool for a Chief Officer. You cannot easily control staff appointments on a financial basis — the question in September "have we enough money left for another teacher at such and such a school" cannot be properly answered. One more teacher's salary may well be within the margin of error in the estimates; repeat the same thing several times and you are not only overspent but committed to more expenditure for the following year.

34. Even so, some thought needs to be given to the definitions involved in a manpower budget. Are the figures quoted to refer to an authorised establishment or to persons in post on a specified day? (in which case there has to be a safeguard against appointments after that day) or do they represent an average throughout the year?; are the numbers of part-time posts to represent the numbers of separate appointments, or should the unit of full-time equivalent be used instead?

35. These questions can be answered — not to provide a completely water-tight system, but to give a sensible guide to staff who may be expected to behave responsibly.

Other Matters

36. We have had to give more careful thought to the build-up of estimates. The general vote headings traditionally put to committee often cover the activities of a number of officers. At some stage it is essential to have a record of the amount available to each officer during the year, and of the amount he has in fact spent or authorised.

37. It followed from this system that the consideration of the routine estimates by the sub-committees became largely a formality. Invariably, in total they exceed the continuation budget, being based on the over-optimistic estimates of heads and principals or branch staff. In due course the Chairmen's Sub-Committee of the Education Committee had to reduce them, and it was at this stage that effective discussion could take place. The more effective debate had in fact taken place earlier in the year when each sub-committee considered its aims and its development proposals.

38. For this system to work best the Council debate should be at a strategic level — on the question of the rate, the balances, the allocation of resources between services. It needs some effort on the part of the Chairman if there is not to be debate on trivialities. The budget should be printed in a form which lends itself to this sort of debate, but Somerset had not yet felt confident enough to

break with the tradition of the large volume of detailed Committee estimates.

Summary

39. It has to be accepted that as a management technique this system can work smoothly, and at a fairly early stage committees can have a reliable idea about their programme for the coming year. But there is a danger that resource allocation depends too much on the officers, and that the allocation to a service can be influenced unduly by the Chief Officer's performance in the Chief Officers' Committee. It is difficult to be detached if a chief officer's own staff regard him as their champion in the lists — but is it not expecting too much of a professional who cares for his service that he should willingly set aside the needs of that service in favour of another? Is it in fact his place to do this? Or is the solution to have detached administrators, who are not emotionally involved, in charge of each service?

40. To what extent has Education been well served by this system? There is some evidence that it suffered in that there was a steady decline in the County's position in the inter-authority league tables. It can be argued that this reflected increased efficiency, consortium buying, and a ruthless weeding-out of unnecessary expenditure. It could equally be objected that the county rate-payers were unduly protected against the effects of inflation by too rigid a control of developments; or that other services were financed at the expense of education.

41. Education was vulnerable too in spending the greater part of the Council's funds. A substantial expansion of, e.g. Social Services could be financed by a small percentage cut in Education —"with a budget of over £30 million you ought to be able to find £100,000 saving". Yet the Education Development Budget was 0.9% of the whole, and £100,000 reduction meant a third cut in that budget.

42. This situation will be worse in the new Counties where Education will spend a higher proportion of the Council's funds than before. The situation is an unhealthy one and may well lead increasingly to the division of the Service into smaller sub-units; alternately continued raiding of what should be Education funds may lead to demands for the removal of Education from the local government system.

43. The question that is left unresolved is this: There has by law to be a national policy for education and the Secretary of State is charged by Parliament with the responsibility for securing the execution of that policy "by local authorities under his control and direction" (Section 1, 1944 Education Act), but:—

44. How does a Secretary of State exercise this responsibility if local authorities claim the right to settle priorities themselves between services?

(v) Coventry's Ten Year Capital and Revenue Budgeting

1. Introduction

The essential rationale of any forecasting or planning system is that by predicting what is likely to happen, some time is made available to respond to the implications of change. In various ways some minor recognition has been given to the validity of this argument but in general practice the tendency has been in local government to deal with an annual budget on a service basis while attention has been given to particular fields of work in *ad hoc* ways. No proper appreciation has been provided of the long term effects of annual decisions nor has there been proper co-ordination of policies. Capital and revenue budget forecasting on a long term basis systematises this approach and provides three distinct advantages which are important in the local government situation. First, it embodies not merely decisions on the allocations of current resources but also estimates of the levels of resources required to secure the maintenance of activities; second, it expresses qualitatively different activities in terms of a common standard of values; third, it enables attention to be directed at the inbuilt commitment of future resources by current plans and standards.

In the course of the last two years the Coventry City Council have carried out their first exercises embodying ten year projections of the capital and revenue budgets. The process pursued in finalising the estimates and settling the rate levels for 1972/73 and 1973/4 yielded a good deal of valuable experience, as well as throwing up a number of problems. A new cycle is proceeding and certain refinements have been introduced. For this reason it should not be assumed that any of the techniques or procedures described below are permanent features of the Coventry scene. Similarly, although various comments on the experience to-date are made below, these should not be taken as implying any final assessment, but rather as pointing ways forward. It must also be recognised that considerable difficulties are being faced in the scale of planning by the very considerable shifts in public expenditure decreed recently by the Government.

Coventry, in common with other Authorities, has been required, under the Town and Country Planning Act 1968, to produce a Structure Plan for the City which deals in broad terms with the social, economic, and physical planning strategies for the next 10-15 years; it was then necessary to elaborate a Local Policy Plan. Basically the Local Policy Plan defines the Council's policies for the whole of the City, states in broad terms how the Council seeks to achieve its objectives and its priorities for doing so. It must have regard not simply to what the Council wishes to do, but also to its ability, as restricted by the resources available to it, to carry out its plans.

Local Policy Plans are divided into district plans, (1), action area plans (2), subject plans (3), and service plans (4).

Since these plans, the Structure Plan and the Local Policy Plan, clearly overlap to a great extent it is desirable not merely that they be compatible but also that they should be produced through the same process. The system of Corporate Management which the City Council is operating and developing seeks to formulate, consider and review on a fully integrated basis all the objectives, policies and programmes. It must be observed that the budget forecasts are elements, albeit important ones, in an integrated approach.

2. The Base Budget

2.1 The Council's ten year capital and revenue programmes are reviewed annually. The main ingredient of each annual review is the base budget, which covers a ten year period commencing with the current year. As the principal objective is to project forward the implications of existing policies in detail, account is taken in the base budget of the following factors:—

2.1.1 the standard and quality of service allowed for in the previous year's budget;

2.1.2 increases or decreases in the numbers of primary and secondary school children, but otherwise the numbers, cases or appropriate units of activity allowed for in the previous year;

2.1.3 the effects of any recent revisions to the approved capital works programme;

2.1.4 the implementation of new legislation;

2.1.5 the full cost of items having only a partial effect in the previous year;

2.1.6 the exclusion of non-recurring items in the previous year's budget;

2.1.7 pay and price levels updated as at November in the current year, thus taking account of the inflation occurring during the course of the previous twelve months.

---

(1) district plans — a series of plans covering each district of the city.

(2) action area plans — plans for areas where there are expected to be intensive changes of redevelopment or new housing schemes.

(3) subject plans — plans which provide detail of a particular issue or project of some magnitude.

(4) service plans — plans for each of the Council's services (e.g. education, social services etc.).

2.2   It should be noted that in the compilation of the base budget, as far as possible, each component of expenditure has been dealt with individually. Although many of the most important factors affecting future expenditure are covered by these guidelines, the precise interpretation of the treatment afforded individual items has led to anomalies in some areas and, more importantly, to the possibility of declining standards in others. Thus, for example, although allowance was made for increasing numbers of secondary school children, no account was taken of increasing numbers of students in further education (other than provision for the succeeding years of established courses and for anticipated contributions to the advanced further education and college of education pools). Again, although allowances were made for repairs and maintenance of premises, they took no account of the considerable school building programme accomplished in recent years nor the ageing of premises. As a third example, though an increased teaching force was allowed for to deal with the larger school population, no corresponding increases were made in supporting staff (physiotherapists, psychologists, careers officer, advisory and administrative staff and so on).

2.3   The main consequence of this approach is that certain increases to the existing level of provision, which might legitimately be regarded as essential, are deliberately excluded from the base budget and must be considered as having a high priority when attention is given at a subsequent stage to possible improvements.

2.4   It must be pointed out that this fault applies to all services e.g. waste collection or maintenance of roads; additional numbers of houses requiring refuse collection or miles of road to be lit and maintained are NOT included in the base budget. If, therefore, such provision is not made in the growth budget present standards could be eroded because the base budget provision has to do a larger job (i.e. service more units).

3.   Programme Review

3.1   The results of the base budget calculations for the ten year period covering all Programme Areas are submitted in June to the Council's Policy Advisory Committee, together with all relevant information, such as the growth forecasts contained in the annual Government White Paper on Public Expenditure; in the light of this the Policy Advisory Committee issues guidelines on the likely level of improvements to be achieved in the following year. On this basis a review of both capital and revenue programmes can be initiated. During the course of this review both service committees and programme area teams (1) play an important role. For example, on the revenue side the Educational Planning Sub-Committee are asked to indicate their priorities from a long list of issues drawn up by the Education Programme Area Team. The items accepted by the Committee are then costed in detail by the Team and alternative levels of implementation are indicated. The Sub-Committee then review the issues and give further instructions as to priorities and levels. (Diagrams 6 and 7 provide further details of the annual cycle). It must be appreciated, however, that the bulk of the work entailed in writing and costing the issue reports falls on the staff of the Education Department.

3.2   During the Review which took place in 1972 this process led to the identification of two categories for consideration with the headings of 'backlog' and 'improvements'. The backlog items were concerned with areas of the service where standards had dropped significantly. Thus the backlog items which eventually received additional financial support included not only repairs and maintenance of buildings and the replacement of furniture and equipment, but certain *per capita* and staffing items. The improvement items which later received some favourable consideration were largely concerned with developments taking place in the pattern of educational need, which required financial input from the Authority if the changes were to be successfully managed. Some of these (for example, the raising of the school-leaving age) were a consequence of national policy, others (for instance, the reorganisation of secondary education, and the provision of educational assistants to reception classes) were consequential to local policy.

3.3   In the following year the Revenue Review process had to take account of the following factors :—

3.3.1   **the provision made in the previous Local Policy Plan for 1974-5 and later years had to be updated** to take account of adjustments made during the year, to bring forward the programme to November 1973 prices and to adjust forward expenditure projections where necessary (e.g. in the light of revised population forecasts).

3.3.2   **the guidance given by the Policy Advisory Committee** Initially the Policy Advisory Committee advised that the overall rate of growth for the City Council should be 8% for 1974-5, excluding inflation with an annual average rate of

---

(1) Programme Area Teams are inter-disciplinary teams of officers responsible for advising Chief Officers on the formulation of policy, for the preparation of plans to meet the Council's objectlves, and for monitoring progress towards their achievement. Each Team is led by a Chief Officer, the Education Programme Area Team being led by the Director of Education.

growth for the ten year period of 5.35%. The rates of growth initially allocated to the Education Programme were 6.73% and 4.04% respectively.

3.3.3 **issues on which the Policy Advisory Committee desired to focus public attention**

Six issues had been selected to be subjects of public participation — the major issue affecting the Education Programme being 'Provision for the Under-Fives'.

Public participation included a series of meetings in the various electoral wards of the city, in which elected members of the City Council were closely involved. Views expressed at these meetings, and in response to questionnaires which were distributed, were considered subsequently in the review of programmes. Special meetings with interested bodies — for example teachers — were also arranged at their request in relation to certain issues.

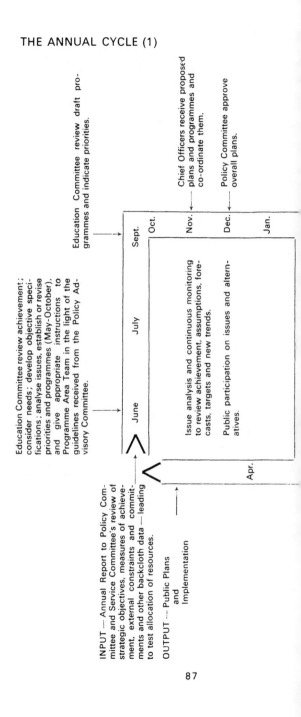

Education Committee review draft programmes and indicate priorities.

Chief Officers receive proposed plans and programmes and co-ordinate them.

Policy Committee approve overall plans.

Sept.

Oct.

Nov.

Dec.

Jan.

Education Committee review achievement; consider needs; develop objective specifications; analyse issues, establish or revise priorities and programmes (May-October), and give appropriate instructions to Programme Area Team in the light of the guidelines received from the Policy Advisory Committee.

June

July

Issue analysis and continuous monitoring to review achievement, assumptions, forecasts, targets and new trends.

Public participation on issues and alternatives.

Apr.

INPUT — Annual Report to Policy Committee and Service Committee's review of strategic objectives, measures of achievement, external constraints and commitments and other backcloth data — leading to test allocation of resources.

OUTPUT — Public Plans
and
Implementation

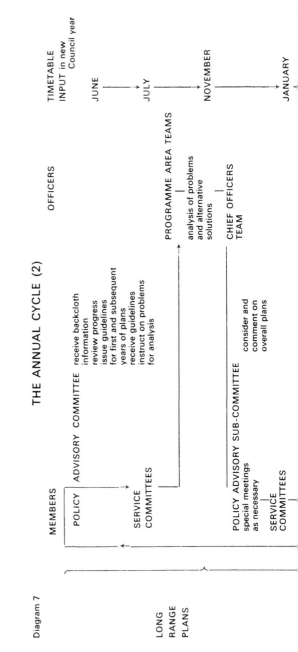

THE ANNUAL CYCLE (2)

Diagram 7

LONG
RANGE
PLANS

3.3.4 **other issues deriving from legislation or other Government initiative**

The White Paper 'Education: A Framework for Expansion' had been published too late for consideration in the previous annual review and the Policy Advisory Committee had decided that the major issues raised should be considered as part of this year's review. These included: nursery education, teacher training, development of higher education, improvements to staffing standards in schools, and replacement of old premises. In addition legislation required the reorganisation of the careers guidance service and developments in further education. Account had to be taken also of the major report which had been published on Adult Education.

3.3.5 **issues identified by the Education Committee as requiring attention**

Some attention had to be given to miscellaneous small aspects of the service, particularly those which were severely affected by inflation but for which no additional resources are provided in the base budget (for example, distinctive school clothing and maintenance allowances).

All the 61 issues contained in (3.3), (3.4) and (3.5) above were costed in detail, with alternative levels of implementation, by the Programme Area Team and advice was obtained from the Education Committee and the Education Planning Sub-Committee on such essential matters as priorities and standards and levels of particular activities.

3.4 The Policy Advisory Committee set aside a week in November or December for discussion of the alternative policies for the city covering a ten year period. In November 1972, for example, the Members were presented with a package of seven plans:

3.4.1 **Budget Forecast**

representing broadly existing commitments including the revenue implication of the approved capital programme.

3.4.2 **Policy Advisory Committee guidelines**

a programme restricted to the guidelines issued by the Committee in the previous June but tempered by advice from Chief Officers that the adoption of this programme would lead to a deterioration in services on a city-wide basis.

3.4.3 **Low Growth**

a combination of all programmes as near as practicable in the opinion of Chief Officers to the Policy Advisory Committee guidelines but without incurring a substantial deterioration in the standard of services.

3.4.4 **Medium Growth**

a combination of all programmes at the medium growth level i.e. an interim stage between high and low programmes.

3.4.5 **High Growth**

a combination of all programmes at a high level, representing the level which Chief Officers in their professional capacities felt to be necessary to meet the needs of the City.

3.4.6 **Social Growth**

a combination of all programmes but giving priority to Housing, Education, Community Health and Well-Being, and Leisure Programmes.

3.4.7 **Physical Growth**

a combination of all programmes but giving priority to Housing, Transportation and Public Protection Programmes.

The Policy Advisory Committee then spent a week (1) studying the proposals for all Programme Areas in detail, together with the appropriate Committee Chairman and with the appropriate Chief Officers.

The package which was finally approved in fact comprised the medium programme for the Education and Community Health and Well-Being programmes and the low programme for other areas but with some small variations.

Having decided on the total plans, detailed budgets were prepared for the coming year for each service.

A summarised statement of the ten year revenue budget approved in November 1972 for the Education Programme is attached (Appendix 1 to this chapter), as also are details of all improvements obtained for the education service, including aspects of the service contained in Programmes other than Education (Appendix 2 to this chapter) for the 1973-4 financial year, as compared with 1972-3.

3.5 Having detailed the mechanics of the Annual Review it may be useful to reflect on the purposes underpinning the process. Given limited financial resources the purposes may be described as —

3.5.1 **estimating and/or reviewing the balance between programme areas** (2)

To ensure, for example, that as far as possible activities with a short planning cycle (such as social services capital projects)

---

(1) In November 1972 the Chairman of the Education Committee and the Director of Education were allocated a morning session for the presentation of the education programme, but in the following year the time allocated was extended to cover a full day.

(2) See the detail outlined on pp. 89,90 concerning the establishment of an initial 'balance'. In subsequent years it is obviously essential that this 'balance' be varied to accord with changing circumstances.

are related to those with a much larger planning cycle (such as major sewerage or transportation schemes) — thus avoiding the latter pre-empting resources which the Council might wish to use in the future for the former purposes;

3.5.2 **enabling the Council to give special support to a particular client group or a particular area of the city by improvements covering a number of Programme Areas.**

Thus the Council can arrange a package deal of 'improvements' constituted to help a particular client group — for example, the under-fives — probably coordinating activities involving all or several services of the Council.

3.5.3 **establishing priorities**

In view of the considerable number of issues where backlogs have accumulated and improvements are thought to be desirable, it is essential to establish priorities; first of all, within individual services and programmes and, eventually, between programmes. The background work of compiling issue papers, attendance at public meetings, consultations with special interest groups, the involvement of Committee members in the consultative process (1) and the putting together of the results of all these activities in the week specially set aside by the Policy Advisory Committee — are vital ingredients in the determination of priorities.

3.5.4 **the revision of standards and levels of service**

One aim of the procedure, obviously, must be to determine those issues where standards appear to be dropping significantly or where changes are taking place in the pattern of need required (2).

3.5.5 **timing and phasing**

the ten year programme provides the opportunity to phase improvements or adjustments over a period of years (for example in the 1972/73 Review the additional monies required to rectify serious deficiencies in the replacement of furniture and equipment were so large that the finance required had to be injected gradually over a four year period). On the other hand an indication that there may be a reduction

---

(1) The consultative process has been outlined earlier in this section.

(2) See Page 85 for a brief outline of the consideration given in the 1972/73 Review to 'backlog' and improvement issues.

(3) See Appendix 1 to chapter (v) on page 98 which summarises the annual effects for the ten year period due to the base budget calculations and the programme of approved improvements in the Review which took place in 1972/73.

of commitment in future years (for example — a decline in the primary school population) may release financial resources for other activities. (3)

4. Capital Programme

4.1 Background

4.1.1 Content

The Capital Programme at present comprises projects, including land acquisition, building construction costs, professional fees, furniture and equipment, which the City Council intend to carry out in the ten years following approval of the Programme in December each year. The first three years represent the Council's 'action programme' (1), and the next two years the 'intermediate programme'. The second five years are presented in less detail than the first.

The three year 'action programme' is a firm programme of priorities for this period and the Council's officers are under a duty to implement the individual schemes. The 'intermediate programme' represents a clear declaration of the Council's intention to schemes in the programme. The content of this programme is more flexible than the 'action programme' but officers are authorised to take action to ensure that schemes are executed in their specific programme year.

All schemes in the capital programme are included in the programme at, and updated annually to, the level of costs current at the date of the annual autumn review. Schemes which were due to start within six months after a review, or which will be the subject of a joint financial report at the immediate pre-tender stage before the next annual review, will be included at the anticipated tender prices.

4.1.2 Programme Review Timetable

A major review of priorities is undertaken each year as part of the annual review of programmes and submitted to Policy Advisory Committee in November, together with reports which assess the financial, manpower and land resources it is anticipated will be required and available over the period. This review incorporates the latest information on the state of readiness of all schemes within the programme.

Interim reviews are undertaken in April and August of each year with the intention, broadly speaking, of bringing to the notice of the Policy Advisory Committee alterations in circumstances or changes in cost affecting individual schemes within the Programme so that it continues to reflect

---

(1) So far as educational projects are concerned the items included in the first three years are usually identical with the 'starts', 'design' and 'preliminary' list approvals made by the Department of Education and Science.

current conditions. These interim reviews will not normally include changes of policy or priority, but they may do so in exceptional circumstances.

4.1.3 Implementation
Implementation of the capital programme is controlled by a system of key dates by which significant stages of a project are required to be completed. The key dates are established by the appropriate Control Group (1). The plan of key dates is then considered by the client department (which is fully represented on the Control Group), by the Capital Programme Implementation Group (2), and later by Chief Officers at one of their weekly meetings. The monitoring of progress, including variation in key dates, is reported through the same channels.

4.2 Ten Year Capital Programme
For many years prior to 1973 the Coventry City Council, in common with many Authorities, had planned its capital programme for a period of five years ahead. As has been explained earlier, so far as the Education input was concerned the first three years of the programme, broadly speaking is restricted to the 'starts', 'design' and 'preliminary' list approvals received from the Department of Education and Science, while the fourth and fifth years are based on anticipations of the approvals likely to be obtained from that Department. Understandably, it is not possible to provide as much detail, or reference to individual projects for the second five years of the ten year programme.

The initial extension of the capital programme to cover a ten year period was undertaken in 1972, following close collaboration with the Housing, City Architect and Planning Officer's and the City Engineer's Departments in order to obtain the best advice possible on future housing developments, including guidance on possible constraints, such as sewerage and drainage problems which may cause the deferment of certain housing schemes for a period of years. Due regard was also given to birth trends and general population trends — a particularly important aspect of which was the fact that numbers in the 18-22 range in the city population were likely to increase by approxi-

_____

(1) Control Groups are inter-disciplinary teams concerned with the implementation of the capital programme. Control Group Leaders are in practice drawn from Senior Officers in the City Architect and Planning Officer's, City Engineer's and City Secretary's Departments.

(2) Control over implementation is coordinated by the Capital Programme Implementation Group consisting mainly of Control Group Leaders meeting under the leadership of the Chief Executive and Town Clerk.

mately thirty-per-cent within the ten year span. Account had also to be taken of the need to replace some old and unsatisfactory premises though, once again, these aspirations had to be restricted to the levels likely to meet the approval of the Department of Education and Science.

Whereas the first five years of the programme comprised lists specifying each individual project, the second five years contained much less detail, merely referring to global sums under the following headings —

4.2.1   Basic Needs

4.2.2   Other Miscellaneous Projects (including nursery, special education, improvement/replacement projects).

4.2.3   Additional Further Education provision.

4.2.4   Minor Capital Works.

4.2.5   Acquisition of sites.

4.2.6   Furniture and Equipment.

A slow decline in the primary school population which was forecast in the post 1975 period seemed to provide the opportunity to envisage a balancing expansion in nursery provision by the utilisation of the accommodation, staffing and financial resources released from the declining primary sector. In anticipation of the publication of the Government White Paper, "Education: A Framework for Expansion", the amounts earmarked for Minor Capital Works in the Council's capital programme were expanded in order to meet an expected increase in nursery education provision. Thus, although the DES allocations for Minor Works were reduced simultaneously with the publication of the White Paper, sufficient allocations were secured locally to begin the approved expansion of nursery education.

The publication of the Government White Paper subsequently, outlining proposals for the expansion of nursery provision, replacement of unsatisfactory premises and expansion of higher education facilities, required, therefore, no amendments to the ten year capital programme established in respect of the Education service by the City Council. Some considerable reconstruction of the ten-year programme in the 1973 review was necessitated by three developments. First, the need to accommodate with the programme a recent decision of the City Council to change the character and extend the two girls' grammar schools so that they could be established as mixed comprehensive schools as from September, 1975. Second, a considerable decline in the births registered in the city had to be taken into account. Finally, some further reconstruction was necessary following the cutbacks in public expenditure announced by the Government and conveyed to Authorities in Circulars 12/73 and 15/73.

5. Commentary

Clearly a considerable number of questions can be raised on the whole approach but it is perhaps worth noting three main points, on the philosophy of the base budget, on its methodology and on the programme review procedures. The base budget only forecasts the implications of current standards. Thus if the annual allocations for the repairs and maintenance of buildings have been inadequate in the past, but the forecast merely perpetuates these inadequacies into the future, then the forecast is misleading and under-estimated. The justifications for the approach so far adopted is that as wide an area as possible should be left open for political decision even though this means, as already noted, that consequently many un-avoidable commitments have to be met from the improvement element. The alternative, that of taking more items into the base budget, implies either a willingness to accept less scope for genuine improvements or the need for more substantial pruning when improvements are to be financed. It is a matter of debate as to where the balance should lie.

As has already been stated the methodology adopted for the base budget gave rise to some inconsistencies in the treatment of various items. Thus, for example *per capita* estimates can be calculated simply by knowing how the school population is likely to change, but the cost of repairs and maintenance of building cannot easily be related to pupil numbers.

Again, although the size of the teaching force can be related directly to pupil numbers, this is not so obviously the case with the supporting staff. On the further education side the difficulties are magnified by much greater uncertainties concerning the levels of participation in college courses, in the youth service, and in adult education where they are so critically affected by factors outside local authority control. These difficulties, which to some extent display the shortcomings of our present techniques, are possibly legacies of the earlier *ad hoc* year to year budgeting. Of course, it should be possible to evolve better yardsticks for such matters as repairs and maintenance. Nevertheless such calculations have not been made because, in practice, this allocation remains a victim of the compromises which have to be made between need and the reality of limited financial resources.

It is fair to say that, although the procedures for conducting the programme review were innovatory on the revenue side, the review followed fairly traditional lines in that only limited analysis on programme budgeting lines was carried out. Experience of the operation of the review and the subsequent estimate preparation suggested also that the procedure imposed new and somewhat different constraints. For example, the main lines of the first annual review had already been settled before the further education college governors could be consulted about their estimate pro-posals; this meant that in subsequent years detailed development proposals concerning the colleges has to be available at a rather earlier stage of the annual cycle than had been the practice. This illustrates the general problem of consultation with other bodies, not only to enable Managing and Governing Bodies to feed in specific recommendations for consideration within the procedure, but to secure some measure of compatibility with the Regional Advisory Council procedures — or at least making allowances for the sensitivities of their position. Here then is a factor which has to be reconciled in the development of systematic planning. Moreover, this is a factor which particularly affects the education service because of the dispersed administration of the service (although the same is also true of the Social Services with their Regional Planning machinery).

Departmental representatives on all Programme Area Teams and other Groups scrutinise very closely the bids being made in the capital and revenue reviews for additional resources, in order to ensure that such schemes are sufficiently substantiated to merit consideration. Otherwise there is a danger that some Programmes may be treated more, or less, generously than others. For example, care has to be taken in all the discussions which take place on the capital programme that everyone concerned is aware of the fact that the education proposals do not relate to the full needs of the service, for they have been pruned already, so that they are either in accord with approvals obtained from the Department of Education and Science or on shrewd assessments of the approvals likely to be obtained from the Department in subsequent years. It must be clearly understood that the basic framework of the capital programme for the education programme has been constructed in this manner particularly if the education proposals are to be compared with the less restricted aspirations which may underlie the bids being made in some of the other Programme Areas.

It is evident that the Local Authority can exert little or no influence on most of the factors determining its future rate of spending (1). Obviously the overall state of the national economy will be a major factor in determining whether the ten year budget is compiled within an optimistic or restrictive framework. Thus in Coventry the Annual Review of 1972 was conducted at a time of reasonable expectancy of the continuous and planned growth in the national economy. As a consequence the approved ten year capital and revenue programmes contained the phasing of most of the aims and aspirations of Committees and Chief Officers within the ten year period.

---

(1)   Factors such as government control of public expenditure, changes in government policies, changes in social attitudes and aspirations, variations in the size and structure of the population, employment opportunities, land availability, the areas in which people choose to live, and the availability of financial resources, including rate support grant.

Unfortunately there is a tendency for many people to assume that items of improvement which are included in year 2 and onwards are firmly committed. It was pointed out earlier (1) that certain capital aspects of the Government's White Paper — 'Education : A Framework for Expansion' had been anticipated in the 1972-3 Annual Review. When these indications of future Government policies in the educational sphere were published, only a few weeks after the local Annual Review procedure had been completed, it was obvious that the implementation of these policies at local level would require some radical reassessment of revenue commitments. The extent of this reappraisal was exacerbated by the Government's published intention to expand nursery facilities and to introduce the teacher education programme fairly near to the beginning of the ten year cycle. Thus, it was evident that some of the 'improvements' which had so recently received approval would not be realisable because of the changed circumstances.

Nevertheless, despite these difficulties and problems, the execution of the capital and revenue budget forecasts has demonstrated not merely the practicability of the exercise, but also its value in indicating the longer term implications of current trends ; one of its particular virtues is that it is a flexible instrument which can readily be adapted in the light of fresh decisions, and it is proving of great value in making adjustments to standards and in forward planning. A good deal of improvement in the techniques used has been derived from the process and this is stimulating improvement in the planning information available. Similarly it is hoped that a more analytical approach to issues will be possible and that this will be carried out on a continuing basis and not merely as part of the annual review. The ten year programme provides opportunities to reflect on changing trends, thus moving away from the previous practice of responding to immediate problems. In these ways more effective managerial control and more rational decision making should be generated.

---

(1) The circumstances appertaining to the present Annual Review are much more frustrating. The worsening nature of the economic situation, culminating in the reductions in public expenditure to the extent of £1,200 million annually will now involve a complete overhaul of the ten year programme and even more restricted notions of what is practicable within this time span will have to be inserted.

EDUCATION

APPENDIX 1 to CHAPTER (v)

Summary Revenue Programme 1973/74 — 1982/83 — Proposals for Expenditure (£'s) (at constant prices)

	1972/73	1973/74	1974/75	1975/76	1976/77	1977/78	1978/79	1979/80	1980/81	1981/82	1982/83
Base Budget	15,647,400	16,554,480	17,278,990	17,925,160	18,259,670	18,541,640	18,820,740	19,014,450	19,219,550	19,402,340	19,613,240
Percentage Increase over previous year		(5.80)	(4.38)	(3.74)	(1.87)	(1.54)	(1.51)	(1.03)	(1.08)	(0.95)	(1.09)
ISSUES:											
1. Capital Programme		28,520	2,990CR	18,380	144,880	376,440	676,960	1,029,200	1,344,720	1,664,730	1,923,100
2. Administrative Support		26,200	30,000	30,000	30,000	30,000	30,000	30,000	30,000	30,000	30,000
3. Repair and Maintenance of Buildings		30,000	135,000	135,000	135,000	135,000	135,000	135,000	135,000	135,000	135,000
4. School Furniture		3,000	120,000	130,000	120,000	80,000	40,000	40,000	40,000	40,000	40,000
5. Library Allowance		2,000	3,420	3,420	3,420	3,420	3,420	3,420	3,420	3,420	3,420
6. Secondary Non Teaching Staff		13,240	22,700	22,700	22,700	22,700	22,700	22,700	22,700	22,700	22,700
7. Maintenance of Technological Aids		15,920	15,920	15,920	15,920	15,920	15,920	15,920	15,920	15,920	15,920
8. Physiotherapists. Psychologists. Home Teacher		6,650	10,370	10,370	10,370	10,370	10,370	10,370	10,370	10,370	10,370
9. Further Education—Technicians		22,750	43,000	43,000	43,000	43,000	43,000	43,000	43,000	43,000	43,000
10. Further Education— Administration		7,620	13,220	13,220	13,220	13,220	13,220	13,220	13,220	13,220	13,220
11. Raising the School Leaving Age		44,360	76,600	76,600	76,600	76,600	76,600	76,600	76,600	76,600	76,600
12. First Year of Infant Schooling		56,590	95,800	95,800	95,800	95,800	95,800	95,800	95,800	95,800	95,800
13. Continuing Courses in Further Education		11,950	20,560	20,560	20,560	20,560	20,560	20,560	20,560	20,560	20,560
14. Grant from Issues 12 and 13		4,450CR	7,900CR	7,900CR	7,900CR	7,900CR	7,900CR	7,900CR	7,900CR	7,900CR	7,900CR

98

Education Committee   Revenue Estimates 1973/74

Provision has been included for the following issues which were approved at the Annual Policy Review:

Education Programme Area	£	£
1. Administrative support — additional staff	26,200	
2. Additional level for Repair and Maintenance of Buildings	20,000	
3. School Furniture additional replacements	3,000	
4. A 20% increase in Library allowances	2,000	
5. Additional clerks and technicians for secondary schools	13,240	
6. A maintenance service and a replacement level of 10% for technological teaching aids	15,920	
7. Additional Physiotherapists, Senior Psychologist and home teachers	6,650	
8. A full year's effect of 7 Further Education College Technicians appointed in 1972/73 and additional posts in 1973/74	22,750	
9. Additional adminstrative staff at the Further Educational Colleges	7,620	
10. Improvements in per capita from "reasonable" to "good" level for ROSLA pupils (2,220), first year Infant pupils (£2,840) and a general increase for schools in disadvantaged areas (£5,000)	10,060	
11. Additional Part-time teachers for secondary schools (£22,170) and teachers for immigrants in Primary schools (£1,200)	23,370	
12. 2nd Deputy Heads in single sex schools Group 10 or over Scores of newly opened/reorganised schools on 4 year forecast	12,250	
13. Extension of Careers service	1,020	
14. A remedial teacher and pilot scheme of educational visitors in secondary schools	5,720	
15. Educational assistants for each Infants school	44,080	
16. Implementation of the Capital programme and continuing the service at the current level	40,470	
		264,350

Health and Social Wellbeing Programme Area (Schools Meals Element)

	£	£
1. Improvements to the buildings	9,000	
2. Replacement of large items of cooking equipment	5,000	
3. Provision of deep freezers	2,000	
		16,000

		£	£

Leisure Programme Area

1. An experimental community use project at one
   Comprehensive and one Primary school — 12,000
2. Additional staffing for the Community provision
   at Sidney Stringer School and Community College — 8,500
3. Additional Adult Education provision — 2,000
4. Charge for part of the running costs of the
   Charterhouse Centre — 5,000
5. Grants to Bardsley and the Diocesan Youth Centre — 1,000
   —————— 28,500

Urban Aid Programme (Authority's contribution)

1. Nursery provision at Wood End Infants School — 2,390
2. Nursery provision at Broad Heath School — 730
3. A play leadership scheme at Little Heath — 380
4. An advisory centre for parents of the Physically
   Handicapped — 680
   —————— 4,180

£313,030

PART V ASSESSMENT OF ACHIEVEMENT

Any management system which depends upon the application of resourses to expressed objectives will need to develop a means of judging how successful that process has been. Assessment of achievement of the education service is extremely complex and there is as yet little general agreement on how this should be done. The following paper attempts to review various pitfalls and dimensions of the subject.

(i) Output Measurement in Education

1. Once upon a time, the Queen appointed a Royal Commission "to enquire into the present state of education in the country....". She had been impressed by complaints that the education provided failed to pay enough attention to the basic subjects and was not sufficiently relevant to the needs of pupils or the community, that too much attention was paid to higher learning and that education was consuming an increasing and disproportionate share of public expenditure especially in view of the low standards and high rate of absenteeism. The Commission reported after three years of collecting statistics and opinions and parts of its report were extracted and implemented. Thus was inaugurated the system of Payment by Results in this country in 1862.

2. At a stroke, a form of output budgeting was applied to the schools by central government. The main elements of this were:

2.1 targets or standards were prescribed;

2.2 schools and teachers were financed to provide education;

2.3 the pupils were examined annually by a government inspector;

2.4 grant was then paid to the Managers, who provided the school and paid the teachers, according to the numbers of pupils who attained the required standard and who had attended regularly.

3. In more detail, the following is a summary of the features of this system:

3.1 Annual grants were paid directly by the Government to Managers of Schools;

3.2 The grants were conditional upon the number and proficiency of the pupils;

3.3 Managers received 4 shillings (1864) per pupil according to the average number in attendance throughout the year;

3.4 8 shillings was paid for each pupil who attended more than 200 sessions and who passed examinations by Her Majesty's Inspector on his annual visits;

3.5 The requirements of the examinations were set out in 6 standards for reading, writing and arithmetic, the first three standards being:

	Standard 1	Standard 2	Standard 3
Reading	Narrative monosyllables	One of the narratives next in order after monosyllables in an elementary reading book used in the school.	A short paragraph from an elementary reading book used in the school
Writing	Form on blackboard or slate from dictation letters capital and small manuscript.	Copy in manuscript a line of print.	Sentence from the same paragraph slowly read once and then dictated.
Arithmetic	Figures up to 20, name and form; add and subtract figures up to 10	Sum in simple addition or subtraction and the multiplication table.	Sum in any simple rule as far as short division.

4. In many ways, we are now discussing the same problem, after allowing for the development over a century, of knowledge, technology, social systems and attitudes and communications. We are experiencing a sense of frustration and disenchantment in our society — not least with and in the education service. Why after 30 years of a sustained high level of investment in education are standards not higher, opportunities more equal? Why are so many of our children (20%) still grossly backward for their age, unwilling pupils, uncivilised? This disenchantment is fed by experience in other advanced countries, such as in the USA, where investment in the innovatory Headstart programme seems to have produced negligible improvement in the development of young children? In backing education heavily to win for a better society has the nation been backing the wrong horse?

Yet, if we are faced with similar criticisms to those of the 1860s, we should beware of similar pitfalls. Contemporary sources of that period provide ample evidence to show that although attendance of pupils improved, the quality of teaching was seriously depressed. Matthew Arnold, H.M.I., wrote in 1867 "I find in English schools a deadness, a slackness and a discouragement which are not the signs and accompaniments of progress. The mode of teaching has fallen off in intelligence, spirit and inventiveness since 1862". In 1876 he wrote: "the great fault of payment by results is that it fosters teaching by rote. In the game of mechanical contrivances the teachers will beat us in the end: by ingenious preparation to get children through the examination without their really knowing how to read, write or cipher". Creativity in teaching was stifled: teachers taught for the tests. Their livelihood, if such a word can be used in this context, depended upon it.

5. If we analyse the system of payment by results, we can distinguish certain elements which are relevant to our considerations of output measurement today. First, measurement (or quality testing) was applied to the product of the system — the pupil. Second, this was done to standards set externally to the schools on a single national pattern. Third, measurement was applied annually. Fourth, measurement was interpreted on the judgement of experts (HMIs) who were also external to the school. Fifth, teachers were used and paid as operatives, rather like production workers in a manufacturing process. Sixth, and of fundamental importance, the education process was treated as a closed system: that is, the attainments of pupils were the direct result of their attendance and the teaching they received at school. The value of this for us today lies not so much in the detail as in the principles of a system of measurement: particularly the following:

6. Nature of the education process
We have seen how measurement in the system of payment by results assumed that the process of education was a closed system within the school. Since then, slow but increasing recognition has been given to the vital influence in a child's development of parents, the family and the community. A child spends about 6 hours a day in school on 190 days in a year, which means attendance at school for 52% of days in a year for 25% of hours in a day. (1). During this time at school he is subject to the influence of the formal education process under skilled staff who are devoted to the development of his knowledge, skills, cultural and social awareness and values. This offers a deliberate and intense developmental experience, which, although claiming a minority of time, is rich in content. The majority of his time is spent outside school subject to the informal influences emanating from the knowledge, values and attitudes of parents, other adults and children, in the family and community. This experience is variable and largely influential at a sub-conscious level.

These informal influences are extremely powerful in the lives of the young. The development of the young child depends not only upon the standards of living but also upon the quality of life within the family and the community. This is being demonstrated increasingly by research studies: for example, the recent studies derived from the National Child Development Study ("From Birth to Seven", "11,000 Seven Year Olds", "Born Illegitimate" and "Growing Up

---

(1) This includes sleeping hours which are influenced by the level of care and comfort surrounding the child.

Adopted"), Professor Bernstein's work on language development or the studies supporting the major education Reports — Crowther, Newsom, Plowden. Similar studies have been made in other countries, particularly in the USA (for example, the Headstart programme and comparisons of the opportunities available to black and white children). All these and other studies show a clear correlation between attainment or development in the formal education process and the circumstances in the informal environment. To paraphrase "From Birth to Seven", at the age of seven, a child from a large family of low economic status from an over-crowded home without some basic amenities (w.c., bath, hot water) is likely to be between a year and 18 months behind the average for his age in reading skills and be an inch shorter in stature. This imprinting of the child by the informal education process has, of course, set in deeply before the age of five, that is, before schooling and the formal process begins. And it is not just a matter of "academic" development; social adjustments, attitudes, values and spiritual, moral and emotional development will also have been imprinted.

It is less fashionable now to talk of genetic or inherited qualities. A child receives a biological endowment from his parents which produces different mental and physical qualities which in turn influence such attributes as physical co-ordination, musical ability, artistic receptivity or creative thinking. These differences must also be acknowledged.

The development of the individual is therefore subject to a variety of influences. Further, the nature and force of these influences are not constant: they vary at different ages and according to circumstances, action, inter-action and re-action. We are dealing with a dynamic situation. It cannot even be simply stated as a relationship between disadvantage in terms of low material and environmental factors on the one hand and below average academic achievement on the other hand. Under-functioning is experienced at all levels of ability and is probably caused as much, if not more, by inhibitions derived from inadequate emotional, spiritual and social development. Much greater attention to these aspects is required in both the formal and informal aspects of education.

Appreciation of these factors is vital to any consideration of output measures in the education service. The education process is not a closed system: the influences of both the informal and formal processes need to be assessed. These are referred to in the feasibility study on output budgeting by the Department of Education and Science (Planning Paper No. 1) as extra-educational (or macro) and intra-educational (or micro) output measures.

7. Time Scale

If the education process can be likened to yeast in a wine-making process, what time should elapse before maturation; when should the first, or best, tasting occur? "Many of the more indirect ways of influencing the education system — such as curriculum development — tend to have a slow cumulative effect. This means that any planning system which is to take full account of the effect of decisions needs to have a long time horizon" (DES Planning Paper No. 1). On the other hand the teacher in the classroom will need to make weekly or even daily checks on progress with individual children and to adjust her programme accordingly. The time scale for measurement must therefore be related to the level, scale and nature of the input.

8. Interpretation

We have seen how in the 1860s interpretation of measurement was the function of Inspectors who were appointed by central government and who were external to and independent of the schools. In effect they had the same role as quality control inspectors or auditors. Is this a proper role and relationship? What is the purpose of output measurement: to provide an effective *control* over activities or to provide *information* for decision-makers? Essentially, output measurement is a tool to assist those who have to make decisions which affect the provision *or use* of resources by providing a better flow of information about the consequences of such decisions and to offer alternative courses of action. Interpretation of output measures is essentially a learning process inherent in the whole planning process: it is not something separate or external to that process. Interpretation of output measures must rest with those who have the responsibility of making decisions and their advisers. The level at which interpretation of output measures occurs will therefore be related to the level at which decision making occurs.

9. Executive levels

The administrative structure of the education service has changed considerably in the last 100 years. In 1860 a government Department of Education administered grants directly to about 6,000 schools which had all been provided by voluntary effort. Today there are three main levels of management:

9.1 *national:* i.e. government level, administered through the Department of Education and Science;

9.2 *local:* i.e. the local education authority of which, from April 1974, there are 104 in England and Wales;

9.3 *institutional:* in 1972 there were 26,072 Primary and Secondary Schools in England and Wales, 1501 maintained and non-maintained Special Schools, 30 Polytechnics, 168 Colleges of Education, 695 Colleges of Further Education and 43 Universities. There were therefore 28,509 major institutions not including youth, community and adult education centres. (It can be argued that there are further levels within the institution such as the whole school or college, the class or course and the individual child or student but these would relate to decisions within the institution).

10. The education service is essentially a partnership and this is reflected in the dispersed administrative structure. The Secretary of State is responsible for promoting "the education of the people of England and Wales" and for "national policy for providing a varied and comprehensive educational service in every area" (1944 Education Act). Local education authorities have a duty "to contribute towards the spiritual, moral, mental and physical development of the community by securing that efficient education shall be available to meet the needs of the population of their area" (1944 Act). The extent of responsibility of Managers and Governors of schools and colleges varies according to the type of institution. In general it can be said that they are responsible for the conduct and efficiency of the institution within the national and local framework. This includes a general responsibility for courses and the curriculum, although in practice in this country, from nursery to higher education, the teaching profession determines the content of the curriculum, subject to the influence of opinion, demand and expectation within society (for example, parents, employers) and by the other partners in the service, particularly examination boards.
It is important to stress this partnership because to a greater or lesser extent each partner has an influence and makes a contribution in the total management situation. These are the levels within the education system at which decisions are taken affecting policy and use of resources. These are the levels, therefore, at which output measures will be used and their use will vary according to the nature and scale of responsibilities.

11. In summary, on the basis of this analysis, we can say therefore that the construction of measures of output or achievement for the education service in this country must be related to the nature of the service and the levels at which decisions are made. In particular the following feature should be respected:

11.1 the multi-dimensional nature of the education process and the need to reflect the influence of both formal and informal educative processes;

11.2 the time scale for the maturation of policies is likely to be a long one but will vary according to the level, scale and nature of the input;

11.3 the dispersed administrative structure which means that decision making occurs at national, local and institution levels.

12. Thus far we have been concerned to analyse the structure of the education service as a background to the use of output measures. We now want to consider the kind of measures which might be

used. It should be emphasised that this is a field where there is little experience on any scale in this country. The following suggestions are put forward in outline only to stimulate discussion. We ask that they are *not taken out of the context of this paper as a whole. We wish to emphasise most strongly the gross misrepresentation and serious harm that could ensue if a single indicator were used in isolation. We have tried to suggest a variety of measures related to different aspects of education. We contend that all of these, and more, will be required as a battery of indicators if any balanced view of the achievements of the service is to be realised.* For example academic achievements must not be considered in isolation from social and other data : a set of results for one pupil, school or area may have a quite different value in relation to the same results in another pupil, school or area. Nothing we say later over-rides this comment.

The following list of some possible measures of output has been classified under types of indicator. Broadly speaking, these may relate either to individuals or a group which will be smaller or larger according to its composition ; for example a whole age group in a school, LEA area or nationally. It is vital to appreciate that the same basic information will have a different relevance or purpose according to the executive level using that information. For example, information on the basis of a whole age group will give a profile of that age group which will allow comparisons to be made with other groups at the same age. Information relating to an individual will provide a profile of the individual and allow comparisons to be made of his standing in relation to his age group. We have only indicated briefly along these lines some of the possible uses the measures suggested.

12.1 Attainment

At school level, a teacher working with a group of children will monitor pupil progress in various degrees and frequencies both on a formal and informal basis. On the more formal basis, this will consist of tests of attainment set by the individual teacher related to class work, assessment (marking) of written work, projects, verbal language, physical activities etc. More informally, the teacher influences the pupil by personal contact, example, personal standards and attitudes, correction, discipline and encouragement. Much of this will be by personal assessment using professional skills and judgement. This monitoring will be accompanied by adjustment of the content and progress of the teaching programme. To this extent, therefore, the teacher carries out his own measurement of achievement in relation to individual children and decides in the light of that what adjustments to make. However, most teachers and Heads want on occasiont to take a comparative judgement of the attainment and potential of a group of pupils against the average for their age. For this purpose standardised objective attainment tests and other tests (for example, of a child's potential or his social adjustment) are often used. It is important to stress that in this context such tests are used for diagnostic purposes to assist the teacher in judging the appropriateness of the teaching programme.

Such tests might also assist the local education authority in its role by the development of cohort testing, that is, by the application of tests to a whole age group. If this were done, say in reading, number appreciation and possibly social adjustment, at the ages of 7, 10, 13 and 15, it would be possible for the Authority, with professional advice, to monitor the standards and trends obtaining in their area and to relate them to the national position for those age groups. Over a period of time, it would assist in assessing the effects of policy or of different "mixes" of resource allocation or levels (for example, the allocation of additional resources to schools serving disadvantaged areas). It might also lead to a further understanding of different types of organisation or method, such as sixth form colleges, open plan primary schools or family grouping.

The Department of Education and Science already carries out regular surveys of reading attainment and the Bullock Committee is currently studying language development and reading standards. If cohort testing were adopted by L.E.A.s, this could be of value at national level. An extension of monitoring in this way would enable the Department to assess national trends (and observe international comparisons?) and regional or subregional differences: other indicators suggest that there are marked variations between regions which are insufficiently heeded in resource allocation.

There are dangers in this. The tests have their limitations in that, for example, they depend upon some acquired knowledge (for example, language) or can be influenced by testing conditions (for example, coaching, health of child, strictness of teachers). There is a danger that some teachers might teach to the tests or that school work would be over-influenced by this. In some areas similar tests are still used to decide the type of secondary education a child shall receive. It is therefore important to distinguish the use that would be made of such tests as indicators of output. They would only be used in relation to individual children by the child's teachers to assist the education process for that child. At local authority and national level they would be used to assist in judging the overall standards of the service and the policy or resource response required.

12.2   Qualifications

The extent to which individuals seek and obtain qualifications through the education service is generally put forward as an obvious and important measure of output. This would include the whole range of standards including CSE and GCE, City and Guilds, National Certificates, graduate and professional qualifications. Information showing the flow of candidates into and out of examination courses and the rates of success or withdrawal from the courses are obviously valuable indicators not only of attainment but also of demand. It would be misleading however to treat such information in such a simple way and other indicators showing the use made and demand for qualifications should be developed. To a certain extent this type of information is becoming available through census and general household survey data, although these may need to be refined in this context. From this type of data we are beginning to be able to indicate broadly the economic (productive input level) and social (individual income level) benefits of various levels of qualification and lengths of courses (i.e. differing investment levels in education). What is also needed is a "satisfaction indicator" from employers which might be developed by survey through the Manpower Commission and Training Boards or by analysis of the amount of additional training and re-training that is required. An analysis of the levels at which qualified manpower is actually employed and the trends in this regard would also be useful.

We need however to respect the limitations and coarseness of grain of such indicators. For example, information about the numbers obtaining 'A' levels at school is useful in itself and, no doubt, also as an indirect indicator of qualities which will be valuable in a competitive world. But we should recognise that such information does not show either the opportunity rate or potential of those who might have taken such courses.

We know from other work (for example, Crowther, Newsom and Robbins Reports) of the close correlation between economic status of parents and level of education attainment. Simple examination statistics can mask the socio-economic constraints on performance.

Clearly such indicators are valuable and to a limited extent are already in use.(1) Their use is likely to be mainly at national and local authority level in application to the decision-making process in strategic planning of higher and further education places and in the distribution of courses. A better flow of information to institutions would however assist their course developments (both in type and content).

12.3   Flow and Satisfaction

Individuals relate to the education service in different ways at different periods in their lives. Between the age of 5 and 16 they are required to be receiving education, usually at school. At this stage therefore, the individual and his parent are in a compulsory or "captured" relationship. For the rest of their lives, the relationship is a voluntary one. The attitudes engend-

---

(1)   See for example the White Paper 'Education: A Framework for Expansion' 1972 — sections relating to Higher Education.

ered within the education service by these two relationships are interesting. It can be said that the compulsory sector tends to be authoritarian while the voluntary sector is more client-programmed. It can also be argued that anyone who enrols for a non-compulsory course or actlvity does so because he wants to. This is an indicator of demand and of success. It is doubtful whether the position is as simple as that or whether sufficient attention has been paid to the interpretation of changes in the flow of numbers in and out of the service and particularly to the motivations of the individuals concerned.

Mervyn King describes in "Social Indicators and Social Policy" (1) the work done at Cambridge University on movements in primary and secondary education. He says that statistics revealing the flow of movements of individuals within the system "correspond more closely to decisions made by the individuals than do statistics of stocks". The extent to which youngsters choose further education or the sixth form or the extent of parents' preference for forms of secondary education including the independent sector at 11 - are other examples. We need to develop such flow statistics further : in relation to special schools and classes, nursery education and playgroups, further, higher and adult education, youth and community services.

Such information does not necessarily reveal satisfaction, and within the compulsory sector there is little general opportunity for such movement. There is a strong case for the development of "satisfaction indicators" at all levels of the service. At least one local education authority is contemplating asking parents on a regular basis to express the extent of their satisfaction with the child's education. This might be extended further to students, employers and employees and also within the youth service by a regular use of sample surveys.

The main use of flow statistics would seem to lie with central and local government in strategic planning but their use, coupled with satisfaction indicators, would be of value in sensitising local institutions to external criteria.

12.4   Social

Apart from passing on and developing the knowledge and skills of society, the education service is concerned with spiritual, moral and cultural concepts and values. The service springs from and is within society. If the primary task of the educator is to release the talent of the individual it is for the use of that talent within society. The service is not therefore pursuing in isolation eternal truths of "the good life" of a civilised state : it must work in relation to the expressed values of the society it serves,

---

(1)   Social Indicators and Social Policy published for Social Sciences Research Council by Heinemann.

although hopefully this will be a creative relationship with the service contributing to social development and confidence. At the same time, the values of an individual are influenced by the interplay of many factors in the community at large. The contribution of the education service in this context will therefore need to be derived from indicators of the "social health" of the community or of the nation generally. In other words to what extent in our society are individuals well adjusted, caring and contributing to the well-being of the community?

The social indicators most applicable to the education service as giving some indication of the "value added" by the service might be of three kinds:

12.4.1 *deviance:* these would be indicative of trends which are considered to be deviant from the general code of law or social behaviour or expressions of personal inadequacy. These would include rates of delinquency, vandalism, truancy and probation among juveniles; crime, divorce, separation and parental neglect among adults; homelessness, unemployment and crime.

12.4.2 *leisure:* it is widely held that education develops its own appetite for learning and culture. Patterns of activity in use of leisure-time should give some indication of the benefits derived from different levels of education. Similarly if an educated person can be disttinguished by his discrimination in use of skill and knowledge, patterns of household expenditure might also be related to levels of education as evidence of the use of judgement in priorities in personal spending.

12.4.3 *adjustment:* we have already suggested the use of tests of social adjustment at school level. These might be developed further for use in further and higher education, the careers service and in employment. Other indirect indicators might be mental health, absence and sickness rates in employment (especially those related to maladjustment).

Such social indicators would be valuable at all administrative levels in the service. Awareness of social factors is apparent within the service in the development of, for example, Schools Council projects on the humanities and the whole curriculum, the concepts of the educational priority area and the vigorous development in a number of LEAs of community education. Further development and more conscious application of this type of information is however required particularly to support co-ordinated planning between health, housing, education and social services.

12.5 Specific Studies

In addition to the development of general measures of output, special studies should be commissioned to evaluate certain aspects of the service or to test policy alternatives. Some bold and valuable work has been done: for example the National Child Development Study and the Halsey Report on Education Priority Areas. There is too a large volume of curriculum development in progress initiated by the Schools Council and individual schools and colleges. Much more research and development work needs to be done however. Over the last 10 years, the DES has developed a research budget but it still (1973-74) amounts to less than £1.5m including its contribution to the Schools Council. The SSRC has only £6m compared with an allocation, excluding capital expenditure, of £60m to the Science Research Council. Research commissions by local education authorities are practically non-existent, although they collectively contribute a total of over £1m to the Schools Council and the National Foundation for Educational Research.

13. We hope this survey will help to show some of the possibilities of applying measures of output to the education service and some of the ways in which this could be of value in decisions affecting policies and the use of resources. We hope we have also shown the need for care and sensitivity in the development and use of such measures. The impact of the service cannot be divorced from other social, economic, and cultural influences. The interpretation of output measures in the education service will need to be done alongside these other indicators.

14. In conclusion we would like to re-emphasise certain factors. Output measurement is not an end in itself and should not be allowed to become so : it is a tool of management to assist decision-making towards a more effective service. Executive levels in the education service are dispersed : the use of output measures should be related to and respect those levels. The education process is diffused and life-long. Single and simple measures will seldom be appropriate : they will need to be correlated with other measures often relating to social and economic factors. The interpretation of such information is a skilled process which should be done under the direction of professional educationists. Attention to these factors is vital if the damage and outside control of activities experienced in the last century are to be avoided and if the benefits of this approach are to be secured for the betterment of the service to the community.

INDEX

117

For Product Safety Concerns and Information please contact our EU
representative GPSR@taylorandfrancis.com Taylor & Francis Verlag GmbH,
Kaufingerstraße 24, 80331 München, Germany

Printed and bound by CPI Group (UK) Ltd, Croydon, CR0 4YY
06/05/2025
01861825-0002